This page is intentionaly left blank.

ISBN-13: 979-8-218-27480-1

A.C. Winklier

THE CONSCIOUS CREATOR'S GUIDEBOOK

The
Conscious Creator's
Guidebook

A.C. WINKLIER

To all those who helped me

and

all those I might someday help

Table Of Contents

How Do I Get What I Want?

How do I get what I want? This is perhaps the most pertinent of life's many pertinent questions. Each and every being who has ever or will ever exist in this world – or in any other for that matter (Martians have needs, too, you know) — will in some way, shape, or form wrestle with it.

The second you left the womb, you began pondering, "How do I get what I want?" You were cold, and wet, and hungry and desperately wanted not to be any of these things. So what did you do? "WAAAAAAHHH-HHHHHHHHHH!!!" You cried. And much to the chagrin of your parents and anyone else unfortunate enough to come within earshot, tears were the primary means of getting what you wanted for quite some time.

As years passed, your methods of fulfilling desires probably grew more sophisticated (I say probably because we all know a few adults who cry just as much as the average toddler). You learned to be nice and to be funny because when people like you, they give you what you want. You learned to work hard and to study up because people who put in the hours get what they want. You learned to intimidate and steal because when all hope is lost, you might as well take what you want and leave the poor bastard whose watch you stole lying bloody on the pavement.

But, whatever your means of acquisition have come to be, you're probably still left wondering — on some level, at least — "But wait, how do I get what I want?"

We all develop methods for getting the objects of our desire, and yet, we've all come to accept that we don't really know how effective those methods are. Some things we get, some things we don't, and most of us learn to live with that. We sit back, half content and half wistful — the few things we have managed to accumulate bring us occasional happiness, and the many things we missed out on are far enough out of mind that we don't feel compelled to cry like babies at our not having gotten them. We put on the Rolling Stones and let Mick Jagger preach to us a fundamental truth of our less-than-fulfilling lives; "You can't always get what you want."

But it doesn't have to be that way.

This is a book about getting the things that you want. In modern spiritual circles, it's become known as manifestation. I like to call it conscious creation. But if it suits you better, feel free to call it what it is — getting things. The content you find ahead is premised on idealism (or a philosophy adjacent to idealism, at least) as opposed to materialism — a point-of-view on which you were probably raised. Basically, our thesis is that you have the power to call objects and experiences that you desire into your life through mind alone.

This may be a totally foreign concept to you; if it is, welcome to a new perspective on the world — it's an honor to be your tour guide today. If you're already well versed in these ideas (maybe you've read Rhonda Byrne's book *The Secret* or dabbled in any number of other spiritual practices that touch on similar subjects), get ready to expand your understanding and start putting theory into practice.

And whoever you may be, rest easy knowing that by the time you finish this book, you'll have all the tools necessary to get everything you ever dreamed of — and you'll be much happier for it.

How To Engage With This Book

What follows are a series of essays all relating back to our central question: How do I get what I want? They're written mostly sequentially, each chapter piggybacking off the previous one, and should probably be read as such — at least initially. Once you've got a feel for the basics, though, feel free to take on each separate idea or essay in whatever order you deem appropriate. Those with extensive backgrounds in all things manifestation or those re-reading the book can probably get away with skipping right to the headier, more esoteric material.

That said, no matter what your experience level, I recommend returning to the early chapters often. The foundational concepts we cover there are — well, they're foundational. If you don't get a good grasp on them from the jump, the rest of what we discuss may not feel actionable. Some concepts are so essential to understand that half the book won't make sense if you decide to skip them. It's important to try and reach some level of experiential understanding of these ideas before proceeding.

I implore you to prove everything I say to yourself before believing it. Manifestation, at its core, is a process of changing how we experience the world.

I appreciate anyone trusting enough to take me at my word when I say things, but that's not a reliable means of making progress. Read everything I write with a critical eye. Ask questions. Expand on my ideas. Take my words and make them your own. The more directly you engage with the material — the more you experiment with it for yourself — the faster you'll move on the path toward manifesting your desires.

One final note: At the back of the book, I'll include two additional sections: one of exercises and one of resources for further study. If you're a person who struggles to make sense of theory alone, try your best to comprehend the essays first, then dive deep into all the exercises. They'll provide you with endless opportunities to put the things you've learned into practice, even if (right now) your perspective is a million miles off from the one being touted. They'll also allow you to build a body of evidence proving that these methods work and are based on fundamental truths of reality.

The resources section will direct you to the teachers and works that guided me on my journey. I'll be referencing different people and works as I go, and that'll be your opportunity to learn more about their points of view or to do more study. My hope is that this is the last work on conscious creation you'll ever have to read, but still, it can be nice to hear people express things in their own words.

And with that, off we go.

Section I:
The Basics

CHAPTER ONE

The Zeroth Principle

The Stanford Encyclopedia of Philosophy defines idealism as a school of thought predicated on the following two theses:

1) Something mental (the mind, spirit, reason, will) is the ultimate foundation of all reality, or even exhaustive of reality, and...

2) ...although the existence of something independent of the mind is conceded, everything that we can know about this mind-independent "reality" is held to be so permeated by the creative, formative, or constructive activities of the mind (of some kind or other) that all claims to knowledge must be considered, in some sense, to be a form of self-knowledge.

Elsewhere throughout history, thinkers have distilled idealism into statements like "all is mind," "as above, so below," and (as new-thought pioneer Neville Goddard put it) "everything is your consciousness pushed out."

The basic thrust of all these definitions is that the "mental" realm precedes the physical one. "Manifestation" is the process by which mentations (thoughts, feelings) find their existence in time and space, i.e., in the physical.

Because the mental precedes the physical — because it's the substrate out of which the physical borrows its form — one could argue that the existence of any independent physical reality is simply an illusion. That mind is the only reality.

This idealistic philosophy is likely a major departure from the materialist perspective in which you've been raised. It is commonly accepted by most people (at least in the Western world) that there exists a physical world into which our individual consciousnesses are born and with which our individual consciousnesses interact.

If a tree falls in the forest and there's nobody around to hear it, does it make a sound? Yes, says the materialist. No, says the idealist.

What's fascinating about the all-pervasiveness of materialism today is that no direct evidence supports it as a valid theory of reality. Any argument made in support of a materialistic point of view by nature can only be backed up by inferred evidence. A simple way to prove this is by investigating the following questions: Have you ever experienced anything that existed outside of your consciousness? Let's take it a step further: Could you ever experience something that exists outside of your consciousness?

The answer to both of these questions should be a quick, resounding "no." Consciousness is the means by which we experience anything. It is a necessary prerequisite for experiencing in the first place. If you aren't conscious, you can't experience. Period.

Some might argue that this point of view is tautological — the fact that consciousness is necessary for experiencing doesn't prove that it precedes the physical world. After all, if individually conscious minds were to arise in a pre-existing physical world, then the world would keep on turning despite any one of the many consciousnesses inhabiting it having been extinguished.

Fair point — perhaps. But to suggest idealism is a tautological way of thinking, yet materialism somehow isn't, is ridiculous. Is it not circular to suggest that if something is experienced, then by definition, there must be a subject experiencing and an object experienced? Again, materialism survives on inference alone. The five senses with which we experience the world require an apparent subject-object relationship.

You clearly are your consciousness — the aware element of your experience. Because you cannot "touch" your consciousness, the experiencing of touch by its very nature requires some form of subject-object relationship. I awareness (subject) touch the tree (object). The same goes for any of the other senses. I awareness (subject) smell the flower (object). And on and on. So, to a materialist, the experience of anything — quite literally, the experience (subject) of any thing (object) — is taken as evidence of a material world consisting of subjects and objects. Because experience exists, a material world external to consciousness must exist, too.

Materialists go as far as to deny the presence of their own consciousness in situations where the subject-object dynamic breaks down. They go to bed at night, sleep deep and dreamlessly, then wake up and say, "I was unconscious." You might be reading that saying, "Yes, they were unconscious," but check yourself before stepping into that trap. In deep sleep, we're not conscious of any thing, yes, but that doesn't mean we cease to be conscious. If we ceased to be conscious in deep sleep, how would we wake up when our wives call our names and shake our shoulders to get us up for work? If consciousness were truly turned "off," those sounds and sensations wouldn't register anywhere. They'd fall on empty ears. The fact that I wake up when my wife calls me is evidence that there's a baseline of consciousness present at all times.

Even having considered all this, if you still want to argue in favor of materialism, have at it. But, for the third time, you're arguing a perspective supported only by inferred evidence. An idealist doesn't have that same problem.

Your consciousness is not inferred. You experience it directly. "I think, therefore I am." Or, as some have argued, the idea Descartes was trying to express, "I am thinking, therefore I exist." I might put it, "I am, therefore I am," meaning "I am conscious, therefore I am." But you get the point.

Idealism is a philosophy supported by the most fundamental truth of all our experience: I am conscious; therefore, consciousness must exist. Beyond that, you can't say much. Anything you're conscious of depends on your consciousness to be experienced. It could exist physically, it could be a hallucination, it could be a dream, etc. All you can say for certain is that consciousness is. It does exist.

So we're going to start there. Consciousness is the fundamental element of all reality. Anything you can experience must be experienced in consciousness and, thus, must be made out of consciousness too. A helpful metaphor for understanding this is children building sand castles on the beach. The sand is the fundamental reality of the beach. The castles children build depend on the sand for their existence, and because sand is the primary reality or substance of the beach, any castle that arises in this reality will be made out of sand.

Consciousness is the only reality.

CHAPTER TWO

Solipsists Eat Alone

When most people think of idealism or hear the statement "consciousness is the only reality," their first inclination is to turn to solipsism: the belief that my individual mind is all that exists and, thus, everything else must be an outprojection or hallucination of my mind. The "brain in a vat" theory conveys this idea succinctly. It proposes that, in theory, you could be an isolated brain in a vat somewhere hallucinating the entire world of your experience — all your family, all your friends, all your memories, all your thoughts, sensations, and perceptions — and the experience would be indistinguishable from the experience of a "real" person living in a material world where all of those things actually exist physically.

This theory is an interesting one (and ultimately, one that can't be either proven or disproven), but it isn't representative of the entirety of idealistic thought. And in my opinion, most people who gravitate towards a solipsistic belief system do so because of a very primary misunderstanding.

When we say "consciousness is the only reality," we have to be very careful not to conflate "consciousness" with "mind." Consciousness is a synonym for awareness — to be conscious is to be aware, but we have to stop right there. "Mind" is a label we've given to things that arise in consciousness but that can't be experienced through any of our five senses.

Thoughts and feelings are not consciousness. If consciousness is the ultimate subject, thoughts and feelings are objects like trees or bikes are objects, just subtle forms of them. Thoughts and feelings depend on consciousness for their existence; thus, consciousness must precede them.

Solipsists make the mistake of differentiating between subtle and gross objects. They see a tree "out there" and have a thought "in here" and assume that the border between subjects and objects must exist at that point — anything that can be experienced through my five senses is an object, anything subtler like a thought or feeling that can't be experienced by the traditional senses must be part of the subject that I am.

But the "person" you likely take yourself to be is an object. We identify with a collection of thoughts, feelings, and images, then organize all our sensations and perceptions in relation to this constructed "ego" and call the whole package our "selves." But this "person" isn't your "self." Your self is your awareness — your pure, unformed consciousness. The person you take yourself to be (in Advaita Vedanta and other schools of non-dual thought, this "person" is often referred to as the "separate self") is an illusion. It's just a container into which you've collected a bunch of subtle objects and then labeled "Me."

We need to understand this to proceed. If we don't, we risk falling victim to the solipsistic trap. When you read "consciousness is the only reality" or "all is mind," don't try to localize your consciousness and see the world as a projection "outward." All is consciousness, yes, and all reality is mental, sure, but the universe doesn't emanate outward from the limited mind of you, John Doe. John Doe the body/mind arises in consciousness or awareness and is made of consciousness or awareness (just like every other thing), but is not the source of consciousness or awareness.

I know I'm going out of my way to hammer this home, but that's only because it's crucially important. When someone says "we are all one!" they don't mean we as individual body/minds are all one (after all, how could we be, when what makes us individuals is the fact that we exist separate from the things around us), they mean we're all one consciousness — or that's what they should mean if they've understood properly. The consciousness that underlies the arising of all our limited, individual body/minds, all the animals, all the plants, all the planets and the moons and the sun and other stars — the same substrate underlies all of those emanations. You are that substrate, and thus, you are everything.

Oftentimes, when people teach manifestation, they use language that implies "you" have a set location in space and are attempting to change the illusory experiences you've projected in front of you. But that's just solipsism — you can call it by different names, yet it's still a belief based on the idea that the "world" emanates outward from me as an individual.

Here's a metaphor I prefer (I first heard it expressed by Ramana Maharshi, one of the progenitors of modern non-dual thought). Imagine consciousness as a movie screen. Everything on the screen — the movie — only exists by virtue of the screen existing first. The movie has no independent existence of its own. If the screen disappears, the movie does too. But, if the movie disappears, the screen remains. So, when you think about the phrase "consciousness is the only reality," don't take that to mean you are the main character in the movie (or the audience member sitting watching the movie) and all the other characters and experiences you encounter are somehow an out projection of your mind — they aren't. You are the screen. The main character exists in your consciousness, but so do all the other characters and things in the world of the movie. And if the movie ends, the screen won't be affected. If the main character (with whom you identify) dies, nothing actually happens to "you" awareness. The movie can still progress, and the other characters can continue existing in the world of the movie. You weren't the main character, even if you thought yourself to be. That was just a misunderstanding.

This description of reality can be incredibly difficult to grasp. There'll be exercises later that help us come to terms with it more easily. But, for now, it may be more helpful to disidentify with the separate self you've taken yourself to be (i.e., disidentify with the main character of the movie) than it is to try and see how everyone and everything else in the world is somehow a projection of your mind. The goal is to understand that what you are, consciousness, underlies your separate self just as much as it underlies the rest of the world.

I could dedicate an entire book to this non-dual understanding of consciousness — I probably should, and maybe one day I will. But for the purpose of getting what we want via manifestation, I think this explanation is enough. Think deeply about what we've discussed here. We've covered the basics of all non-dual traditions. These ideas were preached by Jesus, the Buddha, the Prophet Muhammad, etc, etc, etc. And now you can engage with them, too.

But remember — just because consciousness is the only reality doesn't mean you have to become a self-centered solipsist who denies everyone else their existence and believes their limited mind is the center of the universe. That's not a productive way to live and is based on a misunderstanding of the definition of "consciousness" and the belief that consciousness is something that belongs to each of us individually, as opposed to the screen on which all our lives play out.

Nobody wants to eat lunch alone — but if you become a solipsist, you'll be forced to for the rest of your life, even when the table is full of other people. That's no fun at all, and it's not necessary to manifest the things you want.

CHAPTER THREE

States Of Knowing

In the previous chapter, we took a slight detour off our path. We sparred with the metaphysics of idealism and set the scene for our entrance into the wide world of conscious creation. If the mind-bending stuff hasn't clicked yet, don't sweat it. We've got lots of time ahead. And for now, we're going to cover some general housekeeping.

I want to begin with the term "knowing," as it's one I use often.

"Knowing" is the condition of having accepted something as true at the deepest level of your being. Don't confuse it for belief; it's easy to misinterpret a "knowing" as a belief held with certainty, but really, knowing transcends belief. I believe in Santa Claus. I know I have two arms and two legs. I believe your Father will come back from his trip to pick up milk, even if he left 25 years ago. I know the sun will set tonight and rise tomorrow. I believe I can fly. I know if I can't get my parachute to deploy in the next 15 seconds, I'm going to go splat in that cornfield.

All silliness aside, I hope the point is clear. It might be overzealous to make such a rigid distinction between belief and knowing, as ultimately it's just a semantic difference — but personally, "belief" feels like it has some inevitable quality of uncertainty to it. When we know things for real, we know them. If I were to ask you what kind of car you drive, you'd know the answer instantly. You wouldn't say, "I believe I drive a Honda Civic." Not even "I believe with great certainty that I drive a Honda Civic." You wouldn't say those things not just because only a weirdo gives such mysterious answers to direct questions, but because you know the answer. The car you drive is a fact. If I said to you, "You don't drive a Honda Civic, you drive a Ford Focus!" you'd laugh in my face. Because I'd be wrong. It's not a matter of belief; it's a matter of knowing.

I tend to use the term knowing in place of belief for this reason. This isn't a book about changing beliefs; it's a book about getting anything and everything your heart desires. To manifest successfully, it's not enough to change our beliefs — we have to change the things we know.

To elicit real, meaningful changes in our lives, we need to shift our states of knowing.

States of knowing are like symphonies. Many individual thoughts, feelings, sensations, and perceptions play a part in their makeup. All these specific things are the instruments that come together to deliver your complete concerto of knowing. If I have the sensation of being soaking wet, that's a singular instrument — it doesn't tell me much on its own. Am I swimming in a pool? Did I fall off the edge of the ship into shark-infested waters? Did I wet my bed again?

But add in some pop music, the smell of pizza rolls fresh out the oven, the sight of beach balls bouncing around, the feeling of butterflies in my stomach when the girl I like smiles at me, and the thought, "I hope nobody notices the giant pimple on my nose," — pretty soon I know I'm a 13-year-old at a pool party. The different elements of your experience come together to paint a bigger picture.

You can think about your states of knowing in a general sense or as they relate to your knowing about a specific topic. Everyone has what I refer to as a "primary knowing." This is the lens through which you view all experiences. Some people are pessimists who "know" everyone is a jerk who'll try and rip them off or screw them over. Every room they walk into, they do so with this knowing.

But, that same pessimist might look at his newborn daughter, be filled with love and joy, and "know" that the world is a beautiful place. Just like individual states of knowing are symphonies composed of a collection of individual thoughts/feelings/etc., our primary knowings are composed of all our individual states of knowing.

If 90 percent of your thoughts/feelings/sensations/perceptions are negative, your individual state of knowing will be a negative one. If 90 percent of your individual states of knowing are negative, then your primary knowing will be negative, too.

Keep this in mind as we progress forward into the actual details of manifestation and how to change our states of knowing. Your goal should always be to tip the scales of your individual states of knowing in the positive direction and to start moving your primary knowing to a more positive place.

CHAPTER FOUR

People Are Mean To Me Because I Hate Them

The last basic principle we have to cover combines all of what we've already discussed. When I understand that consciousness is the only reality — that everything, including my "separate self" and all the thoughts and feelings I attribute to it, springs forth from consciousness and is thus made out of consciousness — when I understand that, and I understand that all the thoughts/feelings/sensations/perceptions I experience coalesce into my individual and primary states of knowing, I'm ready to be blessed by the truth that gives rise to all conscious creation. The truth that gives us the power to get anything and everything we've ever dreamed of. That truth is as follows:

My states of knowing underlie (and directly lead to) all of my experiences of the world.

Most people believe the world to function something along these lines — "I feel X because I experienced Y." I feel embarrassed because my boss pulled my pants down at the company Christmas party. I feel angry because my husband cheated on me with his secretary. I feel depressed because I live in my mother's basement and eat TV dinners for every meal.

This is a natural perspective, so you shouldn't feel bad if it's how you've been approaching things for almost your entire life. Still though, despite it being natural, it's a remnant of our having been educated in materialistic philosophy. Now that we've made the leap to idealism (and hopefully, we've made that leap because the shortcomings of materialism are clear), we have to flip our old equation on its head.

"I feel X because I experienced Y" becomes "I experienced Y because I felt X."

That can be a tough pill to swallow. You may be thinking, "Screw off, Dude, I did not choose all the terrible things that happened to me." I understand, and on some level, I agree.

We don't "choose" the things that happen to us. The things that happen to us happen because of the states of knowing we hold.

Get out of the habit of playing the blame game. Nobody is blaming you for any awful thing that may have happened in your life. It's not a matter of whose fault something is.

What I am encouraging you to do is investigate your past experiences and assess honestly whether the feelings triggered by bad things that happened to you *preceded* those bad things happening. I guarantee when you look over your entire life, you will see that a state of knowing (good or bad) existed prior to the experience that seemed to create that state of knowing. Put more clearly, your experiences trigger thoughts/feelings/beliefs/knowings that were already in your conscious or subconscious mind.

As a final point on this topic, when you look for evidence of knowings preceding the experiences that trigger them, don't do so with an overly literal eye. If your toaster broke this morning, that doesn't necessarily mean you've been walking through life "knowing" that your toaster is about to break. You don't have to have the thought, "My toaster is going to break" for your toaster to break. Pay attention to how your experiences make you feel. When your toaster breaks, maybe you feel like crappy things always happen to you and that you can never seem to catch a break. It might trigger a general sense of angst or frustration. That is what you should go looking for in your consciousness. Was the feeling that the experience triggered present *before* the experience actually happened.

CHAPTER FIVE

The Mechanics Of Manifestation

Before we enter the section that'll deal with how to start creating consciously, I want to offer a rundown on the essential mechanism of manifestation. Just about everything you need to know (though knowing it and knowing how to employ it are two different stories), right here in front of you on one single page — I recommend you bookmark this.

Your state of knowing is what manifests. Whatever you want, you need to get in the "knowing" of having before it'll appear in your life. People go on and on about the difficulty "knowing" what it's like to have something they've never experienced having, but it's really very simple.

When a desire arises, what you are actually attracted to is the "knowing of having" your desired object. If it's a hot day and I want an ice cream cone, that desire is born as the knowing of how refreshing and satisfying it'd be to have my ice cream. You couldn't desire any experience if you did not, on some level, "know" what it'd feel like to have that experience. Note — You might not know the specific sensations or perceptions that'll come with your desired experience, but you know how you think you'll feel when you get what you want.

The objects of our desire are just representations of the feelings we're seeking to incorporate into our states of knowing. If I want to drive a race car at Talladega, it's not because I desire the raw experience of driving fast around the track. What I really want might be to feel powerful, free, and exhilarated – the race car at Talladega just becomes the means by which I represent those feelings to myself internally.

If I want to go on a date with the woman of my dreams, it's not because I want the experience of the date alone — what if the date were to go terribly and she was to spend the entire night telling me what an ugly loser I am? Would that be something I'd want? Of course not. I want to feel love, connection, and like I am worthy of being dated by someone I deem to be beautiful. So the date with my crush becomes a representation of those feelings.

You get the picture. If you're very technique-minded and feel like you struggle to access the "knowing" of having your desire fulfilled, then visualization exercises might be your friend. Neville Goddard very famously recommends the "State Akin To Sleep" exercise (aka SATS), whereby you lay down in bed, imagine in vivid detail the experience that you're trying to manifest, and then run the experience on loop all the way through the hazy twilight zone of semi-sleep and into sleep itself.

This is a great method, but any visualization works for accessing your preferred knowing. And really, visualizations aren't even necessary. As I pointed out, if you want something, you already know the feeling of having it. You think you don't because a feeling of lack or not-havingness arises concomantly or immediately after the feeling of having your desire, but just remember why you want the things you want in the first place. Because you know what it's like to have the object of your desire, and what you're trying to do is incorporate that knowing into your larger, primary state of knowing.

When your state of knowing shifts, your experiences will shift to match it. That's the essence of conscious creation.

Section II:
Let's Go
Get Something

CHAPTER SIX

Crawl Before You Walk (Your First Manifestation)

Neville Goddard, the teacher I mentioned earlier, would hold large introductory seminars on manifestation in the 1940s, 50s, and 60s. At the end, he'd offer up a challenge to the room — Go home, and every night before bed, imagine (in vivid detail) climbing up a ladder. Feel it as if it were really happening, and loop the scene over and over again until you fall asleep. Then watch as you end up climbing a ladder in the near future of your normal, waking life. Whether you believed what he was telling you or not, Neville's directive was the same. If you thought he was full of it, this challenge was an invitation to prove him wrong.

Anyone who found themselves climbing a ladder after starting to do the exercise was invited back to the next meeting.

This is an ingenious introduction to manifestation. Climbing a ladder is an experience most people have no preconceived feelings about and no emotional baggage associated with. As such, there'll be few obstacles to manifesting it. Additionally, climbing a ladder is an uncommon enough occurrence that somebody who hasn't climbed a ladder in twenty years then starts doing the exercise and climbs a ladder the next week should be compelled to treat the experience as evidence of the truth of manifestation.

I think the real value of the ladder exercise, though, is that it allows us to crawl before we can walk. In section one, we laid out the metaphysical basis for manifestation — we explained how it actually functions. But that doesn't mean it's easy to take our intellectual understanding and make it experiential. We have to start small and prove to ourselves without a shadow of a doubt that there is evidence of our new idealistic point of view being legitimate.

So, I want to begin by proposing a variation of the ladder exercise.

Here's how it works. We're going to manifest three things. A small household object, the memory of a person we haven't thought about in years, and an experience of uproarious laughter. Let's go through how to approach each of them.

The household object: Pick something that is common in a general sense but maybe not in your own life — for example, a paper clip, a Post-it note, or a mop. If you have a box of paperclips on your desk but haven't seen a Post-it note in years, choose the Post-it note. Remember, we're trying to build evidence for the veracity of manifestation and can't do that if our "manifestation" can easily be brushed off as mere coincidence. At any point during your day (when you wake up in the morning, on your lunch break, before bed, etc.), just bring your chosen object to mind. You can imagine it in picture form, you can visualize picking it up, or you can even just think about the object generally if you have aphantasia or struggle with mental imagery. There are no hard and fast rules here — the exercise will work no matter how you approach it, so long as you're bringing the previously never-thought-about object into consciousness with some regularity.

The person you haven't thought about: This can be anyone. If you're particularly cynical, choose a person with an unusual name. Just like with our household object, bring this person to mind — try and imagine their face, or just think about them and their name — then repeat this process a couple of times a day, every day.

The laughter: Try and remember an experience in which you laughed so hard you couldn't breathe. It doesn't matter what you were laughing about, just that you were laughing and that the memory is pleasant (make it an instance of genuine laughter, not nervous laughter or something like that). Reminisce on this experience a few times a day, just like with the other two experiences we're manifesting. Try and really feel the way you felt in your memory.

Okay. So now we know how to approach the three parts of the exercise. Here's what you'll do next.

Be on the lookout for all three of the experiences you're trying to manifest. You don't have to think about any of them when you aren't doing your exercises, but just keep an eye on the world for them to appear in any way, shape, or form. If you've been thinking about a paperclip, notice if suddenly you find one on your desk when that's not something that typically happens.

And be aware of the subtleties with which these things might appear. Maybe you don't actually pick up a paperclip but are scrolling Instagram when a meme about Clippy from the old Microsoft Word pops up. Maybe you don't run into your old friend Vesuvio in person, but you are in a new town and walk past a restaurant called "Vesuvio's" — anything that triggers the memory of the person is valid. And maybe you don't crack up yourself but are watching a movie when the characters start cracking up, and one of them says, "I'm laughing so hard I can't breathe!"

We're taking a three-pronged approach to the "ladder exercise" for two reasons. Firstly, by drawing three different experiences we rarely think about into consciousness, it'll be difficult to write them off when they all start showing up in your experience. So, as noted earlier, there's an emphasis on gathering evidence here. Secondly (and perhaps more importantly) I want us to learn to be just as aware of subtle manifestations as we are of gross ones. The experience of uproarious laughter is in a totally different class than the experience of picking up a broom. In one case, we're manifesting a concrete object, and in the other, we're manifesting something intangible — an experience.

To get everything you want, it won't be enough to manifest gross objects. You need to learn how to manifest general experiences and desired feelings as well.

The last note I'll make is that the prompts of what we're trying to manifest are intentionally open-ended. I want you to have the freedom to take ownership of your first manifestation. Someone who works with ladders daily won't be sold on manifestation by the ladder exercise. And someone who works from home in their one-story house and rarely leaves might have an intense mental block to the idea of their having the power to manifest climbing a ladder. They might "know" it's never going to work. And we want to avoid approaching our first manifestation from that place. We'll get to manifesting things about which we have intense mental/emotional blocks (that'll be the majority of the book), but when we start out, it's better to start out small.

Crawl before you walk.

CHAPTER SEVEN

Great, I Have A Paperclip. Now What?

Congratulations, you manifested a paperclip! As for what's next? Now you know everything there is to know, and my work is complete. Thanks for reading!

Just kidding.

By starting so early with a manifestation exercise, in some sense, we've put the cart before the horse. That was intentional on my part, as most people are already in a state whereby they can consciously create small things if given a specific directive. But not everyone is there — and even if you are, manifesting a paper clip is an entirely different ballgame than manifesting the love of your life, a million dollars, or a shiny new sports car.

Well, actually, it isn't a different ballgame. The principles of manifestation work the same way in every circumstance, regardless of what it is specifically you're trying to acquire. That's why Neville Goddard called it "The Law" and Rhonda Byrne calls it "The Law of Attraction." Because, in essence, it's a law. It always works and it always works the same way.

So what's the hold-up? Why can almost everyone manifest a paperclip or the experience of climbing a ladder, but almost nobody can say with confidence that they can get anything and everything they want?

The answer is (drum roll please): because of their states of knowing.

Remember our example of being asked what kind of car you drive and immediately knowing the answer? There's a jewel of information in that scenario we haven't thus far mined. You know what kind of car you drive even though you don't go around thinking, "I drive a Honda Civic. I drive a Honda Civic. I drive a Honda Civic," over and over again. But, if when asked, the answer arises immediately, then you must "know" you drive a Honda Civic at all times, even if you're not thinking of it.

Are you starting to see now? Most of your knowing is un- or subconscious. I actually like to refer to it as sub-thought because subconscious implies you aren't conscious of it whatsoever. The exact point we're making, though, is that you are conscious of what kind of car you drive, even if thoughts about it never actually arise in mind.

This is a key distinction, so I'll make it again for emphasis. Most of your "knowing" is sub-thought. It is always present, but it never rises to the level of your thinking mind unless something provokes it. Your mind is limited; it can only hold one thought at a time. Despite this, our states of knowing (both primary and specific) are far more complex than a single thought. So, as an organizational necessity, most of what you "know" hides away in the form of subtle feelings. When someone asks you what car you drive, that's a provocation of your sub-thought "knowing" of driving a Honda Civic. The known fact that has been there all along rises up into the mind so you can speak your answer.

You can effortlessly manifest a paperclip, or a memory of your friend Kieran, or an incidence of intense laughter because baked into your sub-thought knowing is the belief (I know I said I try to avoid that word, but sometimes we have to make concessions for the sake of communication) that it isn't difficult to come across a paperclip, or for something to trigger the memory of your old friend Kieran, or for something to make you laugh hard.

So, it was actually a lie for me to propose the exercise from the previous chapter as an exercise aimed at generating your "first manifestation." It wasn't that at all. It was a tool to further communicate the methods by which we're all manifesting all the time. All you did was call three new things into mind, then let the underlying knowing about them do the job of creation.

This should be inspiring. When you get to the level at which you've mastered conscious creation, that is how easy it is to get what you want. Your states of knowing are so cleansed of limitation and negativity that any experience you'd like to have you call up into mind and it appears in the world, just like that.

Our states of knowing are what manifest. When we coax a knowing up from its sub-thought hiding place and into the mind, we're just catalyzing it. We're speeding up the process by which it manifests in the physical realm.

If you'd never engaged with our revised ladder exercise, you might've still had something trigger the memory of your old friend Janet some years from now. After all, the knowing of her and the knowing of the fact that it wouldn't be the craziest thing for something to trigger her memory is already right there in your consciousness. All the exercise did was give you some power to be more targeted in your approach to turning knowings into reality.

But, our sub-thought knowings are also what keep us from manifesting bigger things. To understand why, and what we can do about it, a brief diversion is necessary.

CHAPTER EIGHT

Releasing

Lester Levenson was born in Elizabeth, New Jersey, in 1909. Despite being raised Jewish in an era of American history rife with anti-semitism, Lester excelled in school and earned himself a full scholarship to Rutgers University to study physics. After school, he worked as a successful physicist, then entrepreneur, operating multiple profitable businesses in different sectors of the economy. As he approached middle age, it seemed Lester was living the American dream. He had a penthouse apartment on Park Ave in Manhattan. He had money, he had friends, he had kind, intelligent women pursuing his hand in marriage — he had most of the things people strive for.

But Lester was unhappy. Then, he had a heart attack. And then another. At 42 years old, the doctors sent him home with a prognosis; there was nothing left to be done. His heart was giving out, and he'd be dead imminently — maybe in a few days, maybe in a few weeks, maybe in a few months, but ultimately, he'd be dead pretty soon. He was even advised to buy a pair of loafers as the stress of trying to tie his shoes might be enough to trigger a final, fatal heart attack.

This event started Lester on a journey of self-discovery that changed his life — and eventually the lives of many others (myself included). I'll include a bunch of material in the resources section for anyone who'd like to learn more about him. And just in case you were wondering, Lester didn't die in a few months like the doctors said he would. He lived until 1994 and never saw another doctor again after his awakening.

One of Lester's key realizations about the human experience was that we all store lots of "junk" in our subconscious minds and that this junk comes to color our experiences and manifest in our lives. This is the same idea we engaged with last chapter. Our states of knowing are populated with tons of content that exists beneath the level of thought, but nevertheless, is always present and always prone to being triggered or called up into the conscious mind.

Our goal when attempting to change our states of knowing is to rid ourselves of our sub-thought "junk" that is incompatible with the thing we're trying to manifest. If I desire a relationship, but have a lifetime of programming telling me I am ugly, unworthy, and incapable of finding love, then my current state of knowing is in direct contradiction with the thing that I want to experience.

Remember, we've switched from the "I feel X because I experienced Y" mentality to "I experienced Y because I felt X." So I don't feel ugly, and unworthy, and all that other garbage because I don't have a relationship, I don't have a relationship because I feel (or better put, because I know) I am ugly, unworthy, etc. Try, though I might, I cannot manifest a relationship in my current state of knowing because knowing manifests as experience, not the other way around. The best I can hope for is a relationship that somehow makes me feel even more ugly and unworthy so long as I maintain my current state.

All that said, what's the solution?

This is the conclusion Lester came to. To rid ourselves of the sub-thought junk that stymies our ability to manifest and makes our lives hell, we need to create a system of taking out the trash, so to speak. And luckily, the system he developed is about as simple as it gets.

All you have to do is face the negative feelings fully, honestly, and without resistance so that you can let go of them. It's called "releasing."

We get into the habit of repressing or burying thoughts and feelings we deem to be negative. My Mom spanks me and I feel like a bad boy who's unworthy of love (probably because while she spanks me, she's screaming, "You're a bad boy, and bad boys get taken to the orphanage if they don't learn to behave themselves!"). I don't like feeling bad, and I don't like feeling unworthy of love, so I'm forced to create a system of repressing that terrible feeling. Maybe I become a people pleaser who does everything in my power to ensure my mother is never again upset at me in the slightest. Maybe I become angry and spiteful — "I'm not a bad boy, my mom is just an evil bitch!" Maybe I do one of a million other things — so long as my solution spares me the pain of feeling bad and unlovable.

But our solutions don't spare us the pain of facing our terrible feelings. All they do is drive our feelings out of our conscious minds and into the jungle of our sub-thought knowing where they'll live in perpetuity. Now, my head might be so filled with angry thoughts that I never have to face my childhood feeling of being a bad boy, but on some level, I've still felt like a bad boy all along. And the second somebody beckons that feeling out of its hiding place — the second they do something that makes me feel like the bad, unlovable little boy — I'm forced to explode into a rage. I employ the solution I've been using since I was a child, and I employ it full throttle because I so deeply don't want to face the way I've felt all along. Then I end up in prison because I punched an old man in the face when he called me a jerk-off for double parking my monster truck.

Luckily, you don't have to end up in prison for punching old men in the face when they trigger your buried feelings. You can just release.

Coax your feeling out of its hiding place, let it up into your conscious mind, then allow it to express itself fully. Don't try to fight it by getting angry or feeling guilty or whatever other coping mechanism you've come to employ. Don't try to repress it by thinking of something else; don't half-heartedly let it out of the jungle in an attempt to speed the manifestation along — just let it shine fully in awareness. It has to be a genuine "allowing." A facing up, once and for all, with the thing you've been afraid of acknowledging.

And when you do that, eventually, your negative feeling will just flow right out of you. You don't have to manipulate it, you don't have to negotiate with it, you just have to face it and face it fully.

Our negative feelings are like little kids who act up for attention. They poke and prod around in our consciousness, and if we smack at them — if we try and drive them out of our conscious, thinking minds with force — while that might be enough to subdue them temporarily, in the end it's just going to make their behavior worse. But, like the misbehaved child, all your feelings really want is to be acknowledged and acknowledged fully. When you give them your genuine, undivided attention and stop resisting them, they'll stop acting up — and unlike a little kid, a feeling will never act up again once you attend to it.

Another metaphor I've used in the past is that buried feelings are like vampires. They die in the sunlight. If you force them away into the shady jungle of your sub-thought knowing, they'll thrive. But the second you bring them into the light of awareness, they'll be burned away.

Get familiar with the releasing process. It'll come to be your most powerful tool on this journey. It's the Swiss army knife of conscious creation.

CHAPTER NINE

Dump Your Bucket First, Fill It Second

Let's say I want a luxury sports car. I lay down in bed and do my SATS. I imagine in vivid detail how the leather seats feel on my legs and back. I run my hand over the steering wheel. I feel the wind blowing through my hair as I rip down the open road. And I fall asleep in the joy of knowing my desire fulfilled.

The next day, I wake up, walk downstairs, and get in my beater 1997 Grand Marquis. I put the keys in the ignition, rev the engine, and then... Poof. My car doesn't start. God dammit.

I call a cab so I can get to work on time. When I climb inside, it's hot and sticky. My driver keeps talking about the surgery his wife's getting for her ingrown toenail, and he's making sure this is the bumpiest ride in history.

About three blocks from the office, we pull up at a red light. I look over and see a guy beside us at the wheel of a brand-new convertible Ferrari. His left hand is on the steering wheel. His right hand is shoved elbow-deep in a bag of cheese puffs. His 90% silicon wife is in the passenger's seat screaming about reality TV, desperately wanting to be heard over the booming bass of the worst song I've ever heard.

"Look at this asshole. Those morons, in that car? Give me a break. They don't deserve it. Who'd he have to rip off to get his hands on that? It's probably stolen. He'll probably wreck it driving like a maniac... Oh my God, look at him! He's getting cheese-puff crumbs all over the leather seats. Hey, asshole! Have a little class, why don't ya?!?!"

The most common issue people encounter with manifestation goes something like this: "I do my SATS and my visualizations every morning and every night. While I'm doing them, I feel great in the knowing of having my desired experience. But then I open my eyes, am faced with reality, and all I can know is lack."

The first problem with this is the idea that you open your eyes and are faced with "reality." As you settle into your new idealistic worldview, the compulsion to delineate between "reality" and the contents of your consciousness will begin to diminish organically. There's nothing we can do to rush that process other than be vigilant in tracing our experiences back to their roots in our consciousness.

For the moment, though, I want to deal with another side of this common complaint. If you do SATS every night for one hour (far longer than most people do it), then you are, at a maximum, in your preferred state of knowing $1/24$ of the time — that's about 4%. This is a great start, and 4% is better than 0%, 1%, 2%, and 3% — but it's still only 4%.

Imagine you have a giant bucket, and you want to use it to mix up a batch of Arnold Palmers. Your end goal is 50% lemonade and 50% iced tea. If the bucket is empty when you start, then this should be easy. Just fill it up halfway with one, then halfway with the other, and you'll be all set.

Now, imagine you start with a bucket that's 75% full with lemonade. You can fill the rest with iced tea, but you won't get your desired mix. You'll have to keep filling the bucket with iced tea, and let the mixture overflow for a while as you pour until you end up with the right balance.

Now imagine your bucket is filled to the top with lemonade, and there's a tap feeding infinitely more lemonade into it at a steady pace — oh yeah, and you decided you don't want Arnold Palmers anymore; you just want to fill the bucket entirely with iced tea. Is it an effective solution to pour an eight-ounce glass of iced tea into the mixture every night before bed? Will you ever end up with a bucket filled entirely with iced tea if this is your method of doing so?

When you employ SATS or any other visualization exercise alone, this is essentially what you're trying to do. Your bucket (state of knowing) is filled with a bunch of crap you don't want and don't need, and the hour a day you put into your exercises is great — in the sense that it does dilute the mixture in your bucket to some degree — but it's not an effective means of changing your state of knowing as it needs to be changed to manifest what you want.

Let's jump back to the sports car example. The hour of SATS I do every night allows me to change the total composition of my state of knowing by 4 percent. If I don't deal with all the held feelings kicking around in my sub-thought consciousness, the best state of knowing I can ever hope for is 4% positive and 96% negative. If I'm really a workhorse (and I don't have a life), maybe I find a way to visualize for 10 hours a day. That still won't tip the scales in my favor.

In reality, the 4% of my day I spend in my preferred state could end up being counter-productive. It might be just enough to bring some more sports cars into my awareness (maybe in the form of advertisements, maybe in the form of the guy next to me at the stop light), but if I haven't dealt with all my negative garbage, then these instances where I see a sports car might end up triggering all my feelings of lack even more so than if I had not done SATS at all.

Releasing is essential because it lets you turn off the tap, empty your bucket, then start filling it fresh. Without releasing, your only chance is to brute force your way into a new state of knowing. That's possible, but requires an almost inhuman level of diligence. You'll have to find a way to access your desired knowing often enough that you make progress in changing the composition of your primary state of knowing. That might look like ten hours a day spent visualizing, or setting a timer to go off every fifteen minutes so you can reassess your desired knowing. Again, this is possible, but why work hard when you can work smart?

If you empty all your junk first, even small progress pays big dividends. If your bucket is empty, then 8 ounces of iced tea a day may not be a lot, but eventually you'll get it filled to the top.

When I'm in the backseat of the cab, and I look over and see the car that I want, I shouldn't get angry or upset or repress my feelings. I should see that as a golden opportunity to release. So I see someone in my car of choice, and it triggers a bunch of sub-thought garbage. Great. I can face it. How do I feel? Like the world is unfair? Like the world is fair, and I'm just a delusional loser for thinking I could ever drive a Ferrari? Like I'll never get what I want no matter how hard I try? That this manifestation stuff is bullshit, and I'm a clown for taking it seriously even for a second?

Face it all. Feel it all. Release it all.

Every time you release, you're emptying your bucket. Every time you repress, you're turning the tap back on and letting it fill even higher with the very stuff you're trying to get rid of.

CHAPTER TEN

Walk Before You Run
(Your First Real Manifestation)

Now you know the basic principles of manifestation and understand releasing, so it seems like as good a time as any for a test.

Pick something that you don't feel requires a Herculean effort to manifest but that, nevertheless, you have some obvious sub-thought aversion to. An example from my own life is finding a good parking space. I used to toil over the difficulty of finding a good parking spot in my city. Anytime I went anywhere, the second I got in my car, there'd be a gnawing in my stomach and a voice whispering in my ear — "Parking is going to be hell." Maybe that's a bit overdramatic, but anyone who's ever lived somewhere with a dearth of good spaces can probably relate to what I'm saying. Parking didn't ruin my life, but it was a regular source of frustration. I'd look up public decks before I went anywhere. I'd leave early so I'd have time to walk to my destination after only being able to find a spot half a mile away. It was annoying, plain and simple.

So pick something like that. Something that frustrates or annoys you with regularity but that doesn't drive you into catatonia — never being able to find a parking spot, your favorite brand of ice cream always being out of stock at the grocery store, whatever.

What I want you to try and do is manifest only by releasing. Don't do any SATS, don't do any visualization. Just release.

Using my example, every time the sense of worry about finding parking would arise, I'd try and release it. Not repress it, not slip into a momentary visualization of finding the perfect spot — just let the feeling up, don't resist, and release it. And I'd do that every time a negative feeling arose until the negative feelings associated with finding a parking space became less and less frequent, then eventually stopped.

You should find that, as you release your negative junk, your desired knowing will manifest without you ever having to actively try and access that state.

I use the parking example because that's something I really was frustrated by and something I dealt with by releasing. And now I am happy to tell you I get parking spots everywhere. I get parking spots on the most crowded streets and in the most packed lots you've ever seen. I get parking spots so incredible that you'd probably want to smack me if you saw them — that is, if you had any energy left after walking 2 miles from your car to meet me at the coffee shop on the busiest street in the city, just to arrive as I was pulling into a spot 10 feet from the door.

And I solved my parking woes by releasing alone. I never did a single visualization. I just emptied my bucket and the spots started coming to me.

CHAPTER ELEVEN

Negativity As A Defense Mechanism

The day after I turned eight years old, I was walking out of school when some of the other boys from my class asked me what presents I'd gotten for my birthday. Excitedly, I began telling them about all my new toys.

Before I could even finish talking, they started to laugh at me. They'd all gotten baseball bats and football jerseys when they turned eight — you know, cool kid stuff — and there I was playing with toys like a little baby.

I'd all but forgotten about this memory until years and years later when I started releasing. Out of nowhere, it just flooded back into my consciousness one day. And I wondered why. In the grand scheme of things, it was an insignificant event. I wasn't outcast or looked down on for the presents I'd received. I remained well-liked, and despite not having asked for adequately athletic birthday gifts as a little boy, I ended up a talented athlete by my teen years. The fact that this strange memory had been hiding out in my consciousness for so long perplexed me.

After thinking about it for quite some time, though, I started to see why it was such a relevant experience. That memory marked the first time in my life (or, at least, the first time I can remember) that I felt compelled to resist my own happiness.

I wanted the toys that I got for my birthday. I was beyond excited to have been gifted them. And despite being laughed at for my interests, I'm sure I walked home and played with my toys joyously. But from that moment onward, I was always unsure if I could trust my own happiness. When the desire to do something "uncool" (as defined by my social group) arose, I felt bad about liking the things I liked, then repressed my happiness in an attempt to pursue more socially acceptable things.

This is a very clear A to B example, but the ways in which we block out our happiness can be deviously subtle. Say you're up for a promotion at work — one you really, really want. You're wracked with anxiety in the weeks leading up to your boss's decision. "Will I get it? Won't I get it? The boss doesn't like me. I'm not qualified. People like me don't get promotions like that." And on and on.

All this negative thinking arises for the same purpose as the "toys are stupid" feelings that arose every birthday after my eighth. They're a defense mechanism put in place to guard your happiness. You feel happy thinking about the promotion you might get. You're ecstatic daydreaming about it. But somewhere along the line, you learned that your happiness needs to be hidden away and protected. So your mind spirals into anxiety, trying desperately to repress the joy you feel. It's almost as if you're saying, "So that I can be happy later, I must fight my happiness now. If I bask in my happiness and things don't work out, I'll be devastated. If I worry now, then don't get what I want, I won't feel a sense of loss."

But our states of knowing are what manifest. So, if all you know is anxiety, all you'll manifest is more anxiety. You might get the promotion, but it'll make you more anxious. You'll spend all your time worrying about losing your job or not having been qualified to get it in the first place. This is how most people live their entire lives. They manifest more and more fear, upset, and anxiety because they think that's the only means of protecting their happiness.

If you let your happiness shine — if you don't fight or bury it — then you'll be in the knowing of happiness. Whatever happens, happiness will manifest. You'll get the promotion and love your new role. You won't get the promotion, but two weeks later, another company will make you an offer at double your current salary.

Be aware of instances when you're dimming your happiness, then take steps to let it shine as brightly as it wants to.

CHAPTER TWELVE

Hunt For Treasure, Not For Traps

For years after I learned about releasing, I struggled to employ it effectively. I'd try and try, sometimes making a little progress, sometimes making huge leaps, and sometimes making none. It seemed to be a difficult process and one that I couldn't rely on to work consistently.

That's because I was doing it wrong.

As previously discussed, negativity arises as a defense mechanism. Our anger and our fear exist to keep us from facing the things we've decided it's better not to face, or as a means of "protecting" our happiness. Negative reactions are the guard dogs of our consciousness. If we stay far away from the deep-seated thoughts and feelings that we don't want to face, the dogs are quiet. You might feel a quiet hum of anxiety, but it won't be particularly painful. The closer you get to the repressed feeling, though, the louder the dogs start to bark. And if you get really close, they'll snap and they'll growl, and they'll make it known, "If you come one step closer, we're going to rip you to pieces."

I used to spend all my time trying to release these guard dogs. Letting my negative emotions up, facing them, and doing everything possible to let them go. But it seemed like no matter how many times I set the guard dogs free, there'd always be more of them popping up when I went back to my repressed feelings. This only happened because I'd misunderstood my goal.

Your goal is not to release your negative feelings. Your goal is to release the thing your negative feelings are guarding from your conscious mind.

Here's an example. Say I have a coworker who pisses me off. He's an arrogant know-it-all. He cuts me off mid-sentence, he doesn't respect my opinions, and all around, he's a jerk. Every time he acts on these traits, I'm hit with a wave of negative emotions. I get angry. Who is he to talk to me that way? What the hell does he know? I do more for this company in a day than he's done in 20 years.

To try and release this anger is possible but incredibly difficult. It's difficult because my angry reaction is downstream from my problem. My coworker's behavior is triggering something inside me — it's bringing a repressed thought or feeling closer to my conscious mind — and the guard dogs are going crazy.

When he talks over me, it might trigger feelings that what I have to say isn't worth hearing — that I'm worthless and expendable. But, because I don't want to admit to myself that I feel this way, I don't. As soon as someone triggers those feelings, the guard dogs I set up get to bark, bark, barking, and I get whipped into a frenzy of anger and frustration.

If you are releasing and painful emotions come up, keep going deeper. The emotions that need to be released are your buried treasure. They're what you're trying to unearth. Any guard dogs, alarm bells, sirens, etc., are actually irrelevant. When you see them for what they are, defense mechanisms, you can walk right past them. Negative reactions and feelings can't hurt you.

Unlike guard dogs, they'll never actually bite. So you don't have to live in fear of them anymore. As you journey down into your consciousness, the alarm bells should come to guide you. If they're ringing louder than you can bear, it means you're almost at the treasure. Don't stop there and say, "Oh no, it's too loud; I can't keep going." Don't freeze and stand there with your hands covering your ears, trying desperately not to hear what you're so clearly hearing. Just dig a little deeper.

When you get to the problematic feeling/belief/knowing, the alarm bells will shut off spontaneously. The defense mechanism you previously set up will have failed. It no longer serves a purpose once you've made it to the treasure; thus, it shuts off.

This is releasing — the shutting off of the alarm bells that occurs when you unearth your repressed feeling. The guard dogs falling asleep and allowing you to enjoy your treasure. It's very unusual when you first experience it because you've spent your entire life setting up a complex system of negative reactions and defenses in order to stop yourself from facing long-ago buried feelings. Then you unearth those feelings and realize facing them isn't even painful at all. It'll be experienced as a neutral feeling. Not even as a feeling. You experience it as a neutral fact. I feel like I don't have anything to say that's worth hearing. I feel unworthy of my job, or of the respect of others.

Is it clear now the distinction between "knowing" and "belief?" Under all our defense systems are the things that we know and don't want to admit that we know. Anything on top of that knowing might appear as a belief: "I believe what I have to say is worth hearing," but it'll never have any power to manifest like those things we know for certain. And, all our negative emotions are just fog obscuring our vision and alarm bells warding us off. When we release for real, and face the knowings we don't want to face, we're 99% of the way towards moving past whatever is limiting us. We've seen our truth and now have the power to change it. But we can only ever change once we're honest about what we know.

CHAPTER THIRTEEN

Release. Release. Release.

At this point, you should be well on your way to consciously creating more efficiently than you ever have previously in your life. If you run into roadblocks in your attempts to release, use the same releasing principle to move past them. Anytime a negative emotion arises, see it as an alarm bell. Find out what it's guarding and go there.

If something seems really hard to release, or if you've been trying to release it, not making any progress, and now you're frustrated, that just means some knowing regarding your power or ability to change is being repressed. You might know that no matter what you do, you'll never have control. Or that fate is against you and nothing can stop it. Your burning desire to understand conscious creation may be arising as a means of repressing those "knowings."

So even if you aren't faced with explicitly negative feelings, something may still be repressed that needs to be faced. Go looking.

In section one, we talked about evidence and how important it is to prove to ourselves that all this conscious creation stuff works. Even more important than evidence, though, is progress. You need to make progress.

That could come in the form of living a happier, more peaceful life or in the form of taking concrete steps toward getting the things you want.

But, if you're stagnant, you have to keep releasing. Dig around for the thoughts and ideas that upset you. Trip your alarms on purpose. Then, dig down to whatever repressed knowing is holding you back.

CHAPTER FOURTEEN

The Big Four: Anger, Fear, Guilt, Shame

As you familiarize yourself with the releasing process, you'll notice a pattern in your emotional defense mechanisms. It'll differ somewhat from person to person, but generally speaking, we all fall victim to a similar set of "archetypal" repressions. Lester Levenson defined a spectrum of emotions, listed in ascending order from most to least destructive, called AGFLAP – apathy, grief, fear, lust, anger, pride. His basic thesis was that different people exist at these different "levels" of consciousness and your level determines how much power you have to enact change in your life. So, someone in pride has more agency than someone in anger, someone in anger has more agency than someone in lust, etc. At the bottom of the list is apathy — think of your classically depressed person, unable to do anything except sit in misery from dawn 'till dusk — the state of zero power.

One of Lester's students, Dr. David Hawkins, created a similar map of consciousness (you can read more about it in his book *Letting Go*, which is part of a fantastic series of spiritual teachings). In the Hawkins model, the lower levels of consciousness are — again, in ascending order — shame, guilt, apathy, grief, fear, desire, anger, and pride.

Both of these systems are incredibly valuable in that they provide a means by which you can assess your primary state of knowing. All you have to do is step back and look at your general state of mind — am I often angry? I'm likely trapped in anger. Am I always anxious and afraid? Must be in fear. And so on.

Remember that when we release, our immediate goal isn't to confront our negative emotions. Ultimately, we'd like to rid our minds of negativity, yes, but negative emotions don't arise in a vacuum — as defense mechanisms they serve a purpose. Acknowledging the purpose your emotions serve is crucial. It's difficult to move beyond them until you recognize why you inserted them in the first place.

Though all the emotions in Lester and Dr. Hawkins' systems are valuable and worth investigating, I want to zero in on four in particular: anger, fear, guilt, and shame. In my experience (both personally and working with others), these four emotions account for a vast majority of releasing troubles. As such, it's worth breaking down how each of them functions as a defense.

Anger is the easiest-to-crack defense system. It is always reactive. Nobody who ever lived felt safe, secure, and at peace while simultaneously being angry. If I find myself in anger, it must be because I feel in danger. I am angry that someone cut me in line at the movie theater? That is a direct product of me feeling afraid I'm at risk of being stepped on, or in danger of not having my needs met thanks to someone else dismissing those needs. Anger is my fight response — you make me feel small, unimportant, or threatened; I don't want to feel small, unimportant, or threatened; I cannot face the way I feel; I decide the best course of action is to lash out and fight back against you. It's the more energetic part of the fight or flight response.

Before we continue, I want to acknowledge something important. Notice how anger arose as a response to fear? There's a reason why Lester and Hawkins ordered their emotional systems in the way they did. As years and years pass, we start to accumulate a debt of repressive emotions. As we drift further and further away from the initial thing we did not want to face, we actually begin repressing our initial repressions. While at first it can be preferable to feel afraid rather than face whatever thought or knowing we don't want to face, at some point, we may decide it's also too uncomfortable to persist in the fear state. As a result, we'll repress our uncomfortable feelings of fear in favor of a more energetic state — often anger, one level higher on the scale. We ascend the ladder, so to speak. This is where releasing can get messy — we may have to trace our path back through increasingly unpleasant states in order to arrive at our treasure — the original thing we felt we could not face. To complicate matters further, once we make it back to the origin of all our repressions, we may start traveling back up the ladder en route to being fully released. So, if I am angry, I may have to trace the anger back to fear, back to grief, back to guilt — and then, once I get beneath the guilt and unearth the thing I was resisting facing in the first place, I might move up into grief, then into fear, then into anger, then into pride, before I get to acceptance.

I don't say this to overcomplicate the releasing process or to make it seem like releasing is a monumentally difficult task. As you become comfortable, you'll be able to cut a direct path to the initially repressed feeling and release it all in one go. But in the meantime, don't be thrown off if it feels like you're moving into lower and lower states as you follow the trail of emotions back through consciousness. Similarly, don't feel like you've failed if you start releasing and don't immediately transition into a state of joyous peace. If you've been conditioned to be a mostly fearful person, as you unload emotional baggage, you might find yourself becoming increasingly angry or prideful — that's okay. You still have work to do, but you're making progress and moving up to a higher energy state.

Now, let's get back to our list. Next up is fear. This is the other side of the fight or flight equation — flight. When there is something we don't want to face, the most natural reaction is often to run from it. This is why anxiety is such a chaotic state of consciousness — because you're running like mad from something you don't want to acknowledge, but not running to any specific destination. This leads to racing thoughts, rumination, etc. Everywhere you turn, you encounter more things to be afraid of. In the moment, this is incredibly uncomfortable, but remember, the very function of fear is to keep you running away from the thing you don't want to face.

Guilt is the level at which it can become difficult to see what purpose your repression serves. It is such an uncomfortable state that it's hard to justify it being preferable to facing some deeper thought or knowing. But still, guilt is a defense mechanism. By burdening ourselves with guilt, in essence, we're trying to beat the world to the punch. We feel inherently bad, but rather than wait for our badness to be exposed and exploited by those around us, we exploit it ourselves. We punish ourselves. Most people are guilt-laden to a tremendous degree. We don't see how guilty we are (after all, most of us repress the guilt further because it's such an unpleasant state) but nevertheless are fighting a constant battle against this emotion. You might find as you investigate that you feel like you've done wrong, even in the strangest situations. I remember going to the Doctor once and being anxious about getting the results of my basic blood work. I was a perfectly healthy young man with no reason to be afraid — so why was I? Well, after analyzing it, I realized what I was dealing with was guilt. I felt guilty for potentially having not taken my health as seriously as I could've (despite my having taken it incredibly seriously). It was almost as if I thought my Doctor would scold and demean me if my scores came back suboptimal. This is guilt, and it shows its face frequently until you learn to address it.

Last up is shame. Like guilt, shame is a more common state than you might think. It's a state of self-hatred. If guilt is an attempt to beat the world to the punishment-punch, shame is our standing up in front of the world and saying, "Yes, I am an evil wretch. Do to me what you will — I deserve it all and then some." Shame is so low energy that its purpose is almost pathetic. Shame is saying, "Maybe if I own up to how terrible I am — if I debase myself in front of you — you won't destroy me." That's the purpose it serves. And again, like guilt, this is such an unpleasant state to remain in that most of us become incredibly adept at avoiding it.

Here's the point of my detailing these four states: in order to make rapid progress in your releasing you have to view your emotional reactions with a clinical detachment. The "conscious" part of "conscious creation" is vital. Become aware of the patterns that dictate how your mind functions. Instead of getting sucked into the whirlwind of negative emotions, see things clearly for what they are. As you learn to see the trends in your feelings, you'll be able to disentangle yourself from the garbage dump of negativity that's holding you back. For every inch of progress you make toward deactivating your anger/fear/guilt/shame defense systems, you'll earn a mile of progress toward your manifestation goals.

CHAPTER FIFTEEN

If Someone Held A Gun To Your Head...

The number one obstacle on your path to effortless conscious creation will be your refusal to admit the success with which you've already been creating "desired" outcomes for your entire life up to this point. Notice the degree of certainty I have in that statement — there are no exceptions to the rule. This was the primary obstacle I had to overcome in my own journey, it's been the primary obstacle everyone I've ever worked with has had to overcome, and it'll be the primary obstacle you'll have to overcome too.

There's a good reason for this. Our refusal to admit past success is not just the biggest obstacle we have to confront — it's the only obstacle we have to confront.

Remember now that conscious creation is not some nifty trick. It's not a magic spell we call upon here and there when we want a shiny new toy. It's an explanation of reality. It's a law of existence. As such, it is immutable. It never ceases to function, and it cannot be bypassed.

Every experience you've ever encountered, you created. And I'm even willing to take things a step further — not only did you create all your experiences, you "wanted" to create them.

Before you write off what I'm saying as an impossibility and start pointing at the laundry list of bad things that've happened in your life (things that, in no way, shape, or form you would or could have *ever* wanted to happen), allow me to explain.

While what we "want" might always seem cut and dry, it really isn't so. I can simultaneously want to lose ten pounds and want to eat an entire box of cookies. I can want to live a more fruitful, productive life and want to lay in bed until noon playing games on my phone. The things that we want often exist in direct contradiction to each other, but nevertheless, we still want them all.

When I say you've "wanted" to create every outcome you've ever experienced, I don't mean you wanted it in any clear or direct way. However, any outcome you ever experienced did have some "payoff" associated with it.

Let me use myself as an example. Dating back almost as far as I can remember, the bane of my existence was what I'd call "political manipulation." People unfairly manipulating situations to ensure their own personal gain at the expense of everyone else. Leveraging money, power, and relationships to secure outcomes they neither earned nor deserved. You can likely think of some classic examples: the child of Hollywood superstars using their name and connections to secure a leading role in some movie at the expense of all the unknown actors and actresses who might've been more talented and more suited to the role. Your coworker using the fact that he's married to the boss's daughter to secure himself a promotion at the expense of you and your coworkers, who might've been more qualified and more deserving of the job.

For the longest time, it seemed no matter where I turned I'd encounter these kinds of political manipulations. I felt forced into positions where any possibility of success depended on my outworking the inherently advantaged manipulators by many orders of magnitude — and note, all this work was just to open up the potential of success. Even were I to work as hard as humanly possible, success was still not guaranteed.

So now I ask, was it really any surprise that I always kept finding myself in situations where the risk of being out-manipulated was serious? Situations where the chips would never fall in my favor by their own volition and where success only came (unreliably) in instances of superhuman effort on my part?

And now, an even more relevant question: Did I not want these situations to occur?

In my conscious mind, I most certainly did not want to continue facing all these instances of manipulation. They were the primary source of stress and suffering in my life, and I wanted deeply to find myself in a position where I was afforded an even playing field.

But on another level, I did want to keep encountering these situations. The belief/knowing at the very core of my personal self was that people are capable of manipulating situations to their own benefit at my expense. This was a fact of my world. And, as a fact of my world, it was something that I both wanted and needed to be confirmed via my experiences.

When something becomes a fact of your world — when a belief becomes a "knowing" — think how essential it becomes for your experiences to manifest in a way that reflects your perspective. Were the world to suddenly stop reflecting the facts we "know" to be true about it, we'd be at risk of our entire worldview disintegrating.

So I ask again, did I not want to continue facing situations where political manipulation was an obstacle? Suppose the world were to stop generating experiences in which I needed to overcome a major disadvantage to be successful, and I were still to end up in a position where I didn't get the outcome I wanted. What kinds of things would I then be forced to face? That I'm not good enough? That I am good enough but so woefully without control over the cruel randomness of the world that nothing I could ever do would bring me closer to the things I wanted?

Which do you think is preferable? To live in a world where you're awesome and talented and have a small chance at success by way of intense effort, or to live in a world where, despite your intense effort, success is almost impossible to come by — either because you're just not good enough or because the world is too uncontrollable?

If someone held a gun to your head and said, "tell me why you've created the life you're currently living and everything that ever happened in it," what would you say?

This is how you have to approach the process of investigating your patterns of feeling/knowing. In order to make progress, you need to arrive at a place of radical honesty — a place of saying, "Not only did I create the outcomes that I've experienced thus far in my life, on some level, I wanted to create them. The bad things that happened in my life had a payoff, and I've been refusing to admit to myself what that payoff was."

There's a great deal of peace in this kind of honesty. You'll suddenly see your life from a place of complete clarity. Everything in your life, in some sense, will be seen as having gone exactly according to "plan." And most importantly of all, the law of conscious creation will suddenly become apparent as the most glaringly obvious fact of your reality. You won't need to trust that everything I'm telling you is true. You'll see that it's true just like you see it's true that the sky is blue and the grass is green.

Until you reach that point, though, conscious creation will continue to be an uphill battle. And it shouldn't be any surprise why. Here I am telling you that creation is a fundamental law of reality, and there you are telling me how you need to learn to manifest so that you can overcome all the terrible, random things that have been thrust upon you by the world. I tell you that not only do we have the power to create what we want, but that this creation process happens effortlessly all of the time, and you tell me that despite intense efforts, you can't stop the flow of negative experiences that are raining down on you all the time.

Admit to your payoff. Anytime you feel like it's difficult to release an unwanted knowing, it's only because you're refusing to face why you inserted that knowing in the first place.

CHAPTER SIXTEEN

Tie It All Together

Congratulations. You've made it. You now know the basic mechanism by which you can get anything and everything you want in life. There are still many odds and ends we'll discuss (the book is far from over), but for all intents and purposes, you've now passed the entry level, intermediate, and advanced courses on conscious creation.

Let's rehash what we've learned as succinctly and clearly as possible.

Everyone exists in states of knowing. There are individual states only relevant to one area of life, broader states relevant to a larger section of life, and all these isolated states come together to form your primary state of knowing — the lens through which you view the world.

States of knowing manifest. So, if you don't enjoy your life, it's because you're holding some knowing that's creating unfavorable outcomes. Our game is to change states of knowing.

How do we do that? We release, then replace. We walk past all our negative reactions and anger, fear, anxiety, etc., then we dig out the treasure that is our repressed knowing. We face it fully, and release it. (Something to note is, when you finally face this repressed knowing, it'll be perfectly clear to you why your life has played out the way it has thus far — you'll see the creation in action).

And finally, once our unfavorable knowings have been let go of, we just insert preferable ones. We stop repressing our happiness. We stop getting lost in the weeds of negative emotions. We make a conscious choice to take on a different knowing. Then we watch our lives change for the better.

Your SATS and your visualizations will be supercharged in the released state. So much so that eventually, I think you'll find it isn't even necessary to use any specific technique or exercise to create consciously. But, at first, you can, and after you've released your garbage it should be very easy to hold your desired state of knowing all day long, even when the visualization ends.

Section III:
Odds And Ends

CHAPTER SEVENTEEN

The Pareto Principle

The Pareto principle states that frequently, in situations with variable outcomes, roughly 20 percent of causes are responsible for 80 percent of consequences. Alternatively known as the 80/20 rule or the law of vital few, it's a principle that colloquially has come to mean a small basis of knowledge can result in a significant deal of results. Even more simply put, when you know a little, you can do a lot.

In sections one and two, we laid the complete groundwork of manifestation. In essence, we did our due diligence in learning the first 20 percent. At this point, (even if it hasn't fully sunk in yet) you basically know everything you need to to manifest successfully. You know the basics of the idealistic philosophy that underlies the conscious creation process, you know that states of knowing are what manifest, you know how to exploit this to manifest little meaningless things, and you know how to release mental/emotional blockages that have thus far prevented you from manifesting all the bigger things that you desire.

The first half of this book should serve as somewhat of an instruction manual. It told you what to do and how to do it, and now you have all the tools necessary to set off and start experimenting. And you should do that. As I said right from the start, your progress will always be tied to the degree to which you engage with the ideas we've discussed and make them your own.

But, as anyone who's ever found themselves sitting on the floor surrounded by random screws, bolts, and mysterious pieces of wood and metal while trying to assemble their Ikea furniture knows, the instruction manual doesn't always take you from start to finish without a single hiccup along the way. You can understand what you're meant to do, but when it comes to actually doing it — to employing what you've learned — there can be a serious learning curve. And to some extent, that's inevitable. I can write page after page of explanation, I can try to iron out every little wrinkle in your understanding down to a microscopic level, and still, you're going to be left with questions. Part of this process is the willingness to toy around with the information you learn until you create a method that works for you.

All that said, this section of the book will be a collection of tips, tricks, and small shifts in perspective that have helped clarify things on my own journey. Basically, it's a journal of insights I've come to after years and years of experimentation. As such, the following chapters won't be quite as sequential as the preceding ones. You can still read them in order, but I'm taking a bit of a shotgun approach and giving you lots of different ideas to mull over and work with. Sometimes, I'll reiterate the same points, just in slightly different ways. Sometimes, I'll reiterate things just because I think they're valuable and worth reiterating. Sometimes, I'll throw out entirely new ideas that came as random bursts of insight, but that don't fit well in any larger narrative or series.

Here's my advice. Treat your manifestation journey like a mountain climbing expedition. In section one, we covered the basics — I gave you all the general details about the mountain you're going to be climbing.

In section two, we familiarized ourselves with the tools we'll be working with most often. Now, in section three, I'll tell you about all the different paths to the summit of the mountain. They all lead to the same point, and you'll need the same basic tools to take on each of them, but some paths will appeal more to you than they do to the next person.

If the way I put something in one essay doesn't click for you, don't sweat it. You don't have to take that path. Pick another one that does work for you. And if all of my different explanations don't do the job, don't sweat that either. You still have all the tools you need to climb the mountain and can blaze a completely new trail to the top.

CHAPTER EIGHTEEN

Work Backward

"I've been doing exercises for x number of days; why haven't I manifested what I want?" "I'm really living in the state of having what I want, but I just never get it."

You see statements like these all over the place — and I spent many years as the person saying them.

Problems arise when you start tricking yourself into thinking you're in the right state to attract what you want but really aren't. Here's an example: I had an old friend who had a negative relationship with one of his coworkers. He needed her help with something, and after some discussion, he resolved to use the principles of manifestation I'd explained to him to get what he wanted. For weeks, he'd tell me how he was sending her loving energy, imagining they were great friends who'd help each other out, and living in the state of having what he needed. Then, after about a month of, he exploded — "All I've been doing is sending this fucking bitch love. I've been doing all the exercises; manifestation just doesn't work for things like this."

If the problem isn't obvious, he was "tricking" himself into thinking he was in the right headspace when he really wasn't. Were you really sending "love" to somebody if you fly off the handle and call them every name under the sun when they don't give you what you want? Were you really living in the end if that's your reaction to it taking more than a month to get what you want?

This is an extreme example, but it's something many of us do. We trick ourselves into thinking we're in the correct state to attract what we want when really we're nowhere close to it.

Here's the solution. Work backward.

Don't be active in telling yourself the state of knowing you're currently inhabiting. Look at the world and your reaction to things that happen, then allow that to show you what the state of your consciousness is.

Been doing exercises ten times a day for three months to manifest some money, then, out of nowhere, you get hit with an unexpected series of bills that drain your bank account even further? *Great.* The world just revealed to you the state of your consciousness. You likely feel that money is hard to come by and harder to hold on to. If that is your default state of knowing, and the manifestation exercises you're doing are just medicine to treat the symptoms (meaning, if you feel like conscious creation is the magic pill to bring you the money that's so hard to come by and so hard to hold on to), then you will not attract money into your life. You'll attract the opposite.

It can be difficult at first to take responsibility for everything you experience in the world. Just remember that conscious creation isn't magic — it's not something reserved for the special few who know about it and can use it to their advantage. Everyone is creating everything in their life at all times. There are no exceptions.

Be relentless in analyzing your experience. It is a perfect map of the current state of your consciousness. Allow it to reveal to you the thoughts and feelings you need to change instead of trying to brute force a new feeling that isn't genuine

CHAPTER NINETEEN

Look To The World For Inspiration

The world is full of successful people and always has been. A small percentage of them may have been educated in the art of manifestation (though they may call it by a different name). The rest just succeeded without knowing even one percent of what we know about conscious creation. What gives? Why is it that you know all about manifestation and struggle to utilize it effectively, but someone else who's never heard a word on the topic has a billion dollars and a garage full of fancy cars?

Manifestation is a law. As such, it continues to function at all times for all people, regardless of whether or not they know how they're using it. There are no exceptions. Once again, this isn't a magic trick a select few can learn about and use to their advantage. It's an explanation of reality.

With this in mind, we must conclude that our mega-successful heroes are all manifesting, but maybe doing so unconsciously. Every rich person manifested richness. Every famous person manifested fame. Everyone in love manifested love.

It can be useful to listen to people you admire talk. Not because what they say will help you emulate their success but because how they say things might. The rich and successful often give clues about their states of knowing when they speak. A common theme you hear is that someone "never doubted" their dreams would come true. You also hear people go on and on about hard work and dedication. What is the belief that underlies a person's commitment to hard work? "My success is closely correlated with the amount of work I put in — external factors can't slow me, so long as I remain dedicated."

Looking at the rich and famous through a magnifying glass can also be valuable. Everyone's experience will have its own subtle flavor — two people could manifest the exact same material conditions, but be in very different states of knowing. Think about all the stars who hit it big, then turned into lunatics when their careers started to wane. To me, that always seems like a manifestation of the belief, "My worth is inextricably linked to the amount of attention I receive." In a case like this, the success a person experiences is actually a manifestation of their deep-seated feeling of worthlessness. It's almost as if their fear of not being enough required they go through a period of getting lots of attention, then losing said attention, so that the fear could manifest in its full monstrosity.

There are endless examples of these kinds of manifestations: The tortured artist whose self-expressions earn them global fame and acclaim, which, in turn, makes them feel even more isolated and alone. The business magnate who feels ugly and unloved, so they set off on a journey to make millions, then wake up one day feeling awful because they're surrounded by people who only love them for their bank account.

A big part of your success in creating consciously will come from attuning yourself to the evidence of manifestation all around you. In some sense, you have to become a seer; you have to learn to see the states of knowing that underlie events occurring in the world. And there are endless opportunities to practice — just listen to people talk, and they'll reveal to you exactly why they live the lives they do.

CHAPTER TWENTY

Your Body Is A Manifestation

Pure consciousness underlies every "thing" that exists in the world. As a result, it must underlie all of our bodies, too. We're so conditioned to identifying with our bodies that we can forget this fact when we first learn about conscious creation. We think manifestations exist outside our bodies and that our bodies are part of our "selves."

Take a microscope to your body as it exists right now. How does it look in the mirror? How does it move? How does it function? How does it feel physically? How do "you" (your mind) feel about it? Do you have aches and pains? Do you keep breaking out in rashes? Are you insecure about your big nose, and no matter how hard you try to hide it, it just seems to keep getting bigger?

The body is a useful tool in the "work backward" system described earlier. By treating our bodies as manifestations in and of themselves, we get a clear glimpse into our states of knowing. How your body looks, feels, and functions is a reflection of your primary state of knowing. Martin

Brofman, the author of *Anything Can Be Healed* (and a teacher I'll direct you to in the resources section), discusses how different physical symptoms are often associated with different personality types. Perhaps the most famous example he uses is the "near-sighted personality." People who are near-sighted physically (who need glasses to see things that are far away) are often "near-sighted" emotionally as well. They don't want to look at things outside of their bubble; they don't easily accept unfamiliar ideas; they don't enjoy socializing with strangers. Basically, they don't want to engage with anything "far away" from them. In Martin's model, physical near-sightedness is a manifestation of mental/emotional near-sightedness. Thus, if you "cure" your mental/emotional state, your physical state will be "cured" as well. You'll be able to see clearly again. The same goes for other maladies.

Now, full disclaimer: I am not a doctor, and nothing I say should ever be construed as medical advice. If you have health issues, always consult with a licensed physician. And I really mean that — I'm not just saying it as a means of legal protection. In many spiritual circles, people "rule out" conventional medicine as if it's somehow inferior to spiritual healing. But as I see it, conventional medicine is a manifestation of health and wellness that stems back through all of human history. Two thousand years ago, if you got an infection, you were done for. But generations of doctors and scientists dedicated their lives to the "knowing" of health, wellness, and life. Their living in these states gave rise to (or manifested) all the incredible medical advancements that we as a species have so far achieved. You'd be a fool to act as if conventional medicine somehow doesn't count as a manifestation because it isn't presented as a magical sorcery. A sick person in 3 A.D. would've considered the manifestation of a single pill that could cure their ailing body a miracle of the highest order.

With that in mind, I don't think it can hurt to go looking for the "knowings" that underlie any physical symptoms. Even things that aren't quite "symptoms" but have to do with the body — like a person who can't enjoy a summer night without getting absolutely ravaged by mosquitos. If that sounds like you, look in your consciousness for some feeling or knowing that might be leading to your bug bite woes. Are you easily annoyed? Do you feel like it's not worth enjoying good things because some little, nagging problem will always ruin your fun? You get the point.

If you analyze your experience and find an obvious state of knowing connected to it, try releasing the negative feeling and see what happens to your symptoms.

CHAPTER TWENTY-ONE

Don't Be A Jerk

When the topic of manifestation comes up, inevitably, there is always at least one person who asks a question along the lines of, "So uhh, can I use this stuff to, like, hurt people?" Despite my opting to write that in as *Beavis and Butthead* a fashion as possible, it's actually not that uncommon a thought, and I'm not casting judgment on anyone who might have had it. But, I would like to clarify why, when you truly understand manifestation, you'll never feel compelled to hurt another person again.

My direct answer to whether or not manifestation can be used to hurt people is, yes — sort of. As we've already established time and time again, manifestation is a natural property of reality. It isn't something that pops up to be used for a specific purpose before the world just goes back to its materialistic baseline, where states of knowing can't influence anything. Everyone who has ever hurt people did so, on some level, via manifestation. The people out there intimidating, bullying, and terrorizing those around them are "manifesting" the pain and suffering of others.

But there's a caveat. In order for someone to do harm to another — for them to manifest your pain and suffering, or for you to manifest theirs —

the victimized party must first accept that others have the power to harm them. Because most people have a primary state of knowing passed down by their parents or their culture, and they don't take steps to actively eradicate their negative knowings via releasing, they (on some level) "know" they are at risk of being harmed by mere virtue of their existence. Even people who live in safe neighborhoods and rarely encounter criminality "know" that the world is an inherently dangerous place and that there are people who might make violent impositions on them.

By the principles of manifestation, for you to harm somebody, they must first "know" that they can be harmed. It just so happens that most of the world "knows" this (I take care to put "know" in quotations because as we've already seen, our "knowings" are malleable and not rooted in any concrete reality).

But that's a little beside the point. What I really want to address is a fatal flaw in the thinking of those who wish to harm others. The desire to inflict suffering is premised on the "knowing" that people are always at risk of being preyed upon and that the best means of acquiring power or control is to acquire it by violent force. More simply put, there is a belief in the world as being governed by rule of "if I don't do it to him, he'll do it to me."

The problem is that this "knowing" sets one up to be preyed upon and made to suffer by others. If you live in a world where the infliction of pain is the only method of getting anything done, then you're unwittingly buying into the belief that someone else might come along and inflict pain on you en route to accomplishing their goals. Have you ever noticed how the cruelest, most crazed dictators always meet the vilest, most painful ends? That's no coincidence. Those dictators "know" violence, rage, and control above all else — they feel as if their ability to be safe and to be happy necessitates their crushing anyone who opposes them. As a result, they always end up being crushed themselves.

If you have any interest in changing your state of knowing to one in which you'll be capable of manifesting misfortune unto others, just know that violence and anger are boomerangs — you can send them out into the world, but inevitably, they're going to come shooting back and crack you in the face.

Skilled creators never wish harm upon others. They recognize that if they hold the "knowing" of harm, then harm will ultimately be done to them. It is much wiser (and far more effective) to always have a "win-win" mentality in trying to get what you want. If I am of the knowing that for me to win, someone else must lose, then by definition, I am at risk of ending up the loser. Nobody has to lose for you to win. When you hold the knowing of love, success, and abundance, you manifest those things for yourself and for everyone around you.

So don't be a jerk – not because it's immoral (it is) or because it's cruel (it is), but because if you're a jerk, then you'll manifest a world full of jerks who'll be happy to step on you like you've stepped on others.

CHAPTER TWENTY-TWO

Take Organic Action

Because manifestation is often thought of as a Harry-Potter-esque school of sorcery, whereby I influence my world via mind and mind alone, people are left wondering if they should take action toward their goals — and, if so, how that action ought to look.

I'd like to begin by saying yes, you can take real, physical action toward your goals and not have to feel as if you're betraying your belief in manifestation. The entire debate regarding whether I should or shouldn't take action in pursuit of my desires is premised on the idea that I, the individual body/mind (I the separate self), am the one in possession of this power to manifest. As previously covered, this is a misunderstanding. Our bodies and minds are themselves manifestations. We, awareness, have the power to create reality, but the separate selves with which we identify are just "avatars" created by consciousness to experience an apparently physical reality.

With this in mind, I say action toward your desires is fine so long as it is the organic action of someone who *will* end up achieving your goals, and not the desperate action of someone who *wants* to achieve your goals but ultimately *will not*. Let me clarify that. If I am thirsty and desire a glass of water, an organic action might be to get up, walk to the kitchen, and pour myself a glass. Getting up and walking to the fridge is a part of the manifestation of my thirst being quenched. Actions like this are perfectly okay to engage in. There's no reason to rule out the "path of least resistance" in your attempts to manifest.

Now, let's look at an example of the two more complex situations: one approached from organic action and one from "lacking" action.

Say I'm a struggling actor. I spend all day making calls to agents, managers, and casting departments in an attempt to earn my big break. I send in a tape for every audition I can find. I do this from the "knowing" that I am going to be the biggest movie star in the world one day. I laugh when I think of the future, where I'll be talking about my journey to success on national television and reminiscing fondly about how hard I hustled at the start. As a result, every rejection I face doesn't bother me — I know I'm not looking for any break, I'm looking for *my* break. The break that ends up making the career of me, the future movie star.

Now on to scenario two. I'm the same actor and I take all the same actions — I make phone calls, knock on doors, and audition for everything. But I hate every second of it. Every rejection stings more than the last, as I "know" my time is running out and I'm moving farther and farther away from my dreams of being a movie star. Sometimes, I break down and cry because I "know" I'll never make it if something doesn't change fast.

We need to be acutely aware of the states of knowing that precede our actions. If you're taking action, but your lack of success triggers some deep-seated negative emotion, you probably "know" lack or failure. On the flip side, If the actions you take are the actions of somebody who will one day have the life you desire, then by all means take them. These actions are just the path of least resistance en route to your goals and shouldn't be turned away from.

If you want to start a business, don't tear your hair out debating whether or not it's appropriate to acquire permits, contact potential investors, etc. Those are totally organic actions and a natural part of your desired outcome coming to fruition.

Again, as noted in our actor example, really any action could be organic action. It's not so much an issue of what you're doing; it's an issue of what compels you to take the actions you do. Be attentive to your inner state and you'll know what the right steps to take are.

CHAPTER TWENTY-THREE

Co-Creation

Many teachings regarding conscious creation and manifestation are so dogmatic when it comes to the idea that "you create your own reality" that they outright encourage delusion as the end game. People in this camp, whether or not they label themselves solipsists, are speaking from solipsistic viewpoint. "The world emanates outward from me, the individual. Every person I encounter is a product of my individual mind. Every situation springs forth from my mind. I, as an individual entity, am God, and the world is my Kingdom."

I think this is a gross oversimplification. While I'd agree we're all capable of creating our own realities (I am writing a book on the subject, after all), the way the process functions is likely a bit more sophisticated than solipsists would have you think.

In section one, we discussed Ramana Maharshi's metaphor of the movie screen. I, consciousness, am the screen on which all appears. I am neither the main character in the movie nor the person in the audience — I am the screen itself. The consciousness that underlies all creation. In thinking this way, we avoid the mistake of fractionalizing awareness. The most accessible conceptualization of the "we are all one consciousness" idea is to treat every individual as possessing their own personal shard of a greater divine awareness. Though all our consciousnesses originate from the same unified medium, we are (at this point in time) separated individuals. I get a shard of awareness, you get a shard of awareness, etc. All our shards are uniform — they're exactly the same — but again, they're separate from each other.

If you operate based on this "shard theory," you'll inevitably encounter a problem. If I create my own reality — if everything springs forth from the divine shard of awareness that I possess — where does that leave everyone else? What about their shards of consciousness? Do they have any power? Is it a creation competition where I must somehow fight to impose my will over everyone elses? Are we all part of a complex system of branching timelines whereby everyone has complete dominion over all versions of their individual lifepath so that I control you in my corner of the multiverse, and you control me in yours?

You could argue in favor of any of these perspectives, but personally, I think the screen metaphor does the job better and with less explanation necessary. As we proceed, remember that it's just a metaphor, and to some degree, we're bound by the limitations of language when we broach the headier topics. Things get funky when we delve into the metaphysics of conscious creation — and the closer we get to a full explanation, the less able we are to conceptualize things in a satisfactory way. That said, we do have some ability to think this through logically,

Imagine first a universe-sized movie screen. All the stars, planets, space debris, etc. are present on it. Everything. Somewhere on the massive screen is the Earth. Somewhere on the Earth, "you," the body/mind (remember, what you really are is the screen) exist. Now, imagine the entire screen has a red tint to it. Red will represent badness and suffering — anywhere red exists (right now that's everywhere), bad stuff is happening. People are hurting each other, people aren't getting what they want, people are unhappy, and so on.

You, as awareness (the screen), have the power to take some portion of the red tint and change it. So, let's draw a small circle around your body/mind and tint it blue (blue represents happiness, good luck, and things working out). Recognize how the blue tint doesn't emanate outward from your body/mind. Your body/mind is in it – maybe it tracks to follow your body/mind as it moves around — but the tint originates from the screen, not the object on the screen.

As you begin to identify more and more as the awareness that underlies all reality, you're gaining the power to tint more and more of the screen (yourself) a desired color. You're expanding the scope of your power by lessening the limitations on your "self." Ascended masters like Jesus or the Buddha were so highly identified — they recognized their true selves to such a degree — that they covered a massive area of the screen in their tint of choice. Their teachings inspire and enlighten thousands of years later and thousands of miles away from where their body/minds lived. Through those body/minds, awareness expressed a larger percentage of its total omnipotence. To even connect their impact to their body/minds misses the point; they had such monumental impacts on the world *precisely because* they transcended their limited body/minds.

I recognize this might be getting too convoluted to follow, so allow me to make my point. The reason conscious creation is able to function is not because our individual body/minds have any agency of their own. The main character in the movie doesn't have any power to direct the plot. But, as consciousness, we are capable of directing the action on the screen. We can cast whatever tint we like over some portion of the screen, creating an entire eco-system of body/minds who experience positive outcomes.

This brings us to the title of our chapter, co-creation. Though I as a body/mind do not possess the power to make you as a body/mind act according to my will, if I am standing in the light of positivity, you (by default) will enter into that light upon our interacting. When you access your desired state of knowing, you cast a specific tint on your immediate world and anyone who steps into your world. Again, this doesn't mean everyone will necessarily give me what I want immediately — but the people I end up encountering will be those who are meant to stand in the same light as I am. Those not meant to stand in my light will either never enter it, or they'll move through it without a trace — the exposure to my tint may have been something they needed to experience on their journey, but they'll leave no lasting impression on the tint as I experience it.

Here's another metaphor meant to clarify co-creation. Imagine a particle accelerator. You, awareness, are the scientist setting the course of a particle (your body/mind). Depending on the speed and direction you fire off the particle, it will interact or insect paths with different particles inside the accelerator. So co-creations are just the ways in which we intersect with other body/minds en route to our desired outcome.

Understanding co-creation won't necessarily have an impact on your immediate manifestation process. It doesn't provide much actionable information that you can use to redirect your thinking. What it does provide, though, is another means by which to check your state of knowing. If you're constantly encountering people who rip you off or screw you over, you must be participating in a co-creation. You're standing in the light of unfairness and injustice, playing the role of the preyed-upon victim. The person who scams you is standing in the same light, playing the other role. If you stand steadfast in your desired state — if the light takes on a different tint — that same person who used to screw you over might be perfectly just when you interact with them. They might continue to screw everyone else over, but never have any problems with you. Or, they could naturally fade out of your life — the lights in which you stand might just be incompatible.

Above all else, never forget that you, as awareness, have full power to choose the light in which your body/mind stands. Never feel compelled to step into someone else's darkness. They don't have any power to force you down to their level. And in all likelihood, they'll gladly accept the opportunity to step into your shining light.

CHAPTER TWENTY-FOUR

Advice For The Anxious Minded

A lot of people I work with, especially in the early stages of their learning about conscious creation, spiral into anxiety because they're afraid every thought they have will now manifest in reality. What if I manifest my family members getting sick? What if I manifest an accident? What if I manifest my boyfriend leaving me for the woman I'm jealous of?

If this sounds like you, allow me to assuage your fears. Remember that our states of knowing are what manifest. How those knowings express themselves in thought is largely irrelevant. If you live in a totally anxious state of mind, the world you manifest will, at worst, be anxiety-inducing. Once a bad thing happens, the anxiety surrounding your anticipation of the bad thing disappears. If your partner leaves you, all remnants of the fear that your partner will leave are immediately neutralized on account of the event having actually taken place. Quite literally, that specific anxiety can no longer exist.

THE CONSCIOUS CREATOR'S GUIDEBOOK

In this way, anxious states of mind tend not to result in noteworthy manifestations. Because, were something noteworthy to occur, the anxiety could no longer persist. Again suppose you're anxious about your partner leaving you. You might manifest them coming home just slightly suspiciously late one night ("she was supposed to be here 30 minutes ago, could she be cheating on me?") or maybe you'll manifest a strange reaction that makes you say, "is he losing interest in me?" but that's about the worst of it.

If you're in the midst of anxious thinking, this probably won't be all that comforting. But at minimum, it should clarify for you that states of knowing are what manifest and that the knowing of anxiety is very different from the knowing of a bad thing happening. So, you don't have to worry about accidentally cursing yourself because you had one intrusive thought. If conscious creation worked that way, everyone who's ever thought, "I should probably hustle through this crosswalk, people drive fast on this road..." would be flattened out on the pavement somewhere. Anyone who'd ever worried about anything would've been forced to see that worry actualized completely.

The last note I'll make about anxiety has to do with a point I glossed over earlier. When you're anxious about something bad happening, then the bad thing happens, your anxiety disappears in an instant. Sure, you might remain anxious about other things, or maybe your anxiety about your partner leaving was a small part of a much larger anxiety that nobody will ever love you, but when something specific occurs, it immediately becomes impossible to remain anxious about that thing occurring. Does that immediate dissolution of a negative emotion sound familiar to you?

Yes. It all ties back to releasing. If you acknowledge the knowing that your anxiety is trying so hard to keep you turned away from then your anxiety will shut off. You can face up to the thing you've been running from, and it'll fade away too without ever needing to manifest.

Section IV:
Beyond Conscious
Creation

CHAPTER TWENTY-FIVE

Where Do We Go From Here?

Once we understand manifestation and can employ it to our benefit, we're left with an important question: Where do we go from here?

What's next for a person who can get anything and everything they want? Is that the end of the story? Will we all just fade away with the setting sun, ever content to play with the endless toys we've created for ourselves?

Mastering manifestation isn't the end of the road, existentially speaking. Learning to get the things you want is a spiritual rite of passage — that's why so many religions, philosophies, and other schools of thought dedicate time to discussing it. But once you have the things you want, it's time to start considering what it is you need.

Section four is all about the bigger picture. To some extent, it might be sacrilege to dedicate an entire section of *The Conscious Creator's Guidebook* to issues extending beyond conscious creation. Still, if what I've written thus far has been successful in providing you a means to manifest anything and everything you want, then you'll probably end up needing some guidance on how to take the next step in your journey. So, without going too far out of bounds, the following essays will give you some things to think about. And someday, another book might be in order — one that gives these topics the full attention they probably deserve.

CHAPTER TWENTY-SIX

What Do You Really Want?

When people are asked which objects and experiences they desire, responses will vary. I want a big house and a shiny car. I want a wife and kids who love me. I want a camper van so I can tour the American West. I want some peace and quiet. Everyone will be different, and every answer is a valid one.

But what's the common thread? If all this stuff can be classed as desirable by different people, there must be something shared between it.

That something is happiness.

It might seem obvious at first glance, but it actually isn't obvious to most people. Everything you ever have desired, everything you desire currently, and everything you will desire is the same thing. You desire happiness.

Sure, how we define happiness might differ. And certainly how we represent happiness to ourselves will. But below it all, what you desire is happiness and happiness alone. Here's a way to prove it: take an object or experience you desire (a new job, a nice car, the perfect husband) and imagine I'm a Genie who could grant that wish with a snap of my fingers. But, as is the case with Genies, my granting your wish comes with a hidden cost. You'll get the thing you desire, but it'll make you miserable.

Your car will run like crap and break down within a week of you buying it. The repairs will cost thousands. Your perfect husband will turn out to be a lazy narcissist who never does a second of work around the house but has no problem berating you from dawn 'till dusk. Your life will suck, but you'll have the things you wished for.

Sounds great, right? I hope not.

We desire the things we desire because we think they'll make us happy. If we knew for certain they wouldn't make us happy, we'd stop desiring them. And for the few of you saying, "I'd still desire what I desire, even if it were certain I'd end up miserable," you're desiring happiness too, just a subtler form of it. You feel as if you can't live without your desired object/person/ experience, so (in your eyes) having it and being miserable would still be a movement *toward* happiness — even if happiness were never achieved.

Our brains aren't good at extricating happiness from the imagined experiences we think will make us happy. Here's another example to communicate that. Imagine again that I'm a Genie. I can grant you eternal happiness right now, but once you receive your wish, you'll spend the remainder of your life living alone in the woods, never bathing, and eating bugs and worms for every meal. You'll live to 100 years old, in perfect health and vitality the entire time (and you'll be euphorically happy), but will never leave your woodland paradise. Think you'd take this offer? I doubt it.

But why is that? Your complete happiness is guaranteed. You'd be as happy as any person ever could be — happier than anyone ever has been. So why does everyone have a gut reaction of "No way, dude." In an attempt to settle the cognitive dissonance, people will drone on and on about how the true goal of life isn't necessarily happiness, but fulfillment, or interaction, or not eating worms for every meal. This is all just the mind's attempt to explain its unexplainable aversion to a deal it can't make sense of.

The real reason nobody would take this offer is that our expectations of what will make us happy are incredibly deep-seated. They formed decades ago. They were imposed on us by our parents and our society. They were set in motion long before we were even born. Get a good job and you'll be happy. Marry a nice girl and you'll be happy. We have a deep intuition about what will or won't make us happy — so when I propose complete happiness, health, and fulfillment in exchange for a lifetime rolling around in the mud eating worms, everyone's answer is essentially "No, because I couldn't be happy living like that."

I'm not advising you to go live in the sticks and eat grubs for sustenance. Some spiritual sects advise a strictly ascetic lifestyle, but I don't think that's necessary to live a beautiful, fulfilling life. Becoming a hermit doesn't drive anyone closer to enlightenment.

What I do suggest is that you work hard to see how happiness is not in the objects and experiences you desire. Happiness is in you. I represent happiness to myself via the sports car or the fancy house, but those things don't have any happiness "inside" of them. Happiness is not an inherent quality of any object or experience. You are happiness (an idea we'll discuss in the following chapter).

This is important. Understanding it allows us to look objectively at our desires. Do I want to be a Doctor because medicine is what I'm truly passionate about, or do I want to be a Doctor because my parents have told me for 20 years I *should* want to be one? Do I want my abusive ex-boyfriend back because our relationship will work out this time, or do I want him back because I feel alone and worthless, and even were he to continue abusing me, if we were together, at least I wouldn't feel alone anymore?

You deserve the best. You deserve complete happiness without the slightest tint of sorrow. And your desires should be in line with that.

CHAPTER TWENTY-SEVEN

Desire Fulfilled Is Your Natural State. You Are Happiness

When a long-standing desire of yours is fulfilled, how do you feel? You might say happy, excited, or at peace, but that's not quite what I mean. I'm not talking emotions here. I mean, how do you feel in a more fundamental sense? What changes when your burning desire is finally fulfilled? Because something must change, right? If nothing changed, your desire being fulfilled would be a non-experience. You wouldn't feel compelled to satisfy desires if their attainment didn't shift something about your life. So again, I ask, what changes?

If you're struggling to come up with a concrete answer, that's a good thing. Because there isn't a concrete answer. Nothing changes when a desire is fulfilled, except that the desire fades away.

Desire fulfilled is your natural state. Happiness too, is your natural state. In fact, what you are is happiness. This is why we don't feel like a different person when we get something we want. On the contrary, we feel *more like ourselves*. When we're happy, we feel as if we're finally living in our true, natural state. A state that we may have forgotten for some time, but upon returning to it, a state that strikes us as deeply familiar.

I know this can seem a little abstract, so let's clarify. Say I want a sports car. We know from earlier conversations that what I really want is happiness, and I choose to represent that in the form of a sports car. I get my sports car, I am happy, and my desire for the sports car dissolves into nothingness now that I've acquired the object I wanted. So what am I left with?

It's easy to treat the process of fulfilling a desire as a transaction. I trade my desire for the happiness inherent to my desired object. But a transaction isn't actually taking place. I don't exchange my desire in return for happiness. Really, what's happening is, I get my desired object, my desire fades away, and I'm left with... well, I'm left with nothing. I'm left with myself. And when I'm left with myself, I experience what we've labeled "happiness." But happiness is just the experience of myself, free from the bondage of desire and negative emotions. So all along, I was happy. Desire just blinded me from that fact.

It is no coincidence that freedom is one of the highest human values. People have been fighting for freedom since the dawn of time. One of man's greatest evils, slavery, is evil precisely because it's the oppression of another's freedom. The most heinous crimes like rape and murder are crimes of freedom too — one infringes on another's bodily freedom or even their freedom to live.

To be free is natural. When we are free from all negativity and desire, we call it happiness. When we are free from judgment and insecurity, we call it love. Though sex is often engaged with for reasons other than love, when it's practiced in a truly intimate way, it frees us from our separation from another. Quite literally, a unification of bodies takes place. Enlightenment is the freeing of one's self from the limitations of the body and mind — it's a permanent reunification with everything and everyone. It's the ultimate freedom (Lester Levenson actually referred to it as such).

Here's why we get into all this. Though we vest our happiness in people, objects, and experiences, that's not where it actually exists. It is inside us, or more accurately, it is us. Your desires are clouds blocking out the sun that is your infinitely happy self. Releasing is the holy grail of conscious creation for this reason. When we release our fears and negativity and desires, we're clearing the sky of the pesky clouds that are obscuring the happiness and love of our being.

Remember this next time you feel far away from happiness or from whatever thing you've been trying to consciously create. You aren't. No matter how many clouds are in the sky, the sun always shines just as brightly.

CHAPTER TWENTY-EIGHT

But If I Let Go Of My Desires...

Letting go of your desires will not lead to you never obtaining them, but just not caring. Let me say that again — if you let go (or release) your desires, that does not mean you'll never attain them. It also doesn't mean you will attain them, but not enjoy them. And finally, letting go of desires does not mean you have to be content in desirelessness, forever twiddling your thumbs (albeit happily) in a rocking chair somewhere.

Many people are averse to releasing for these very reasons. They think they're being tricked. I give up my desire, and now in my new desireless state, life sucks just as badly as it did before, but that doesn't bother me. Or, I give up my desires, then I do achieve them but can't enjoy them because I'm a zen zombie. That's not how it works. I promise you. This isn't a trick.

When you start to release, some desires may fade naturally. This is just a consequence of having realigned your perspective. If you'd been desiring a reunion with the woman who spent years abusing you, then ran off with the mailman, releasing might lead to that desire falling away.

But this desire only falls away because it was, in the first place, a defense mechanism. You felt worthless and unloved when she left, couldn't face that, and then began hyper-fixating on winning her back. But you didn't want her back for how sweet and loving she is; you wanted her back because her choosing to be with you would make it easier to ignore your inherent feelings of worthlessness.

But true, positive desires don't dissolve when you start releasing. Francis Lucille, a phenomenal advaita vedanta teacher, talks often about life as a celebration. In the aforementioned example of wanting your abusive wife back, there is no celebration happening. Your desire isn't borne out of love and connection, and reuniting with your lover won't be a celebration of intimacy and bliss. That desire is just a means of further repressing the feelings you don't want to look at.

But imagine sitting on a tropical island, listening to the waves, feeling the sun on your chest, and thinking, "You know what would be great right now? A nice, cold glass of lemonade." You're not desperate for the lemonade. Your desire isn't born out of a sense of lack and suffering. Wanting a cool drink is just an expression of the peace and relaxation you already feel. It's a celebratory desire. And celebratory desires manifest very easily. Before you're even done having the thought, a waitress might come by with a glass of lemonade, free of charge. Or, a random beachgoer might pass by with a cooler in tow — "Hey, we're heading back to the hotel now but have some drinks left over. Would you like one?"

When you live life as a celebration, things manifest in all sorts of ways, and it requires no effort. But again, this is not the same thing as having nothing and not caring about it. When you start to release, you'll have more stuff than you ever did previously; it'll be nicer stuff, and you'll appreciate it more.

CHAPTER TWENTY-NINE

Why Do Bad Things Happen?

If everything is consciousness, and consciousness is God, then why do children die? Why did awareness bring the Holocaust to manifestation? Why do bad things happen at all?

You'll encounter a range of answers when you ask these questions in spiritual circles. God has a plan, we're told, even if we can't understand it. Because everything that could ever arise in consciousness finds its manifestation in some form eventually (after all, consciousness couldn't be the all if we were able to conceive of some experience that couldn't arise in it) horrible things have to happen just as often as good things. Suffering is the point of life — only by overcoming suffering do we gain the spiritual strength necessary to ascend to higher and higher states.

I think all of these responses have some merit. It's true that we have to recognize the limitations of our human minds (remember, minds arise in consciousness and do not encompass the totality of consciousness by their lonesome) and not write off what we don't understand as inherently nonsensical. Furthermore, yes, it is true that since consciousness is every-thing, everything will find manifestation — good, bad, or otherwise. And finally, there is wisdom in our recognition that struggles — even of the most intense sort — can provide an opportunity for growth.

But I don't think that paints the entire picture. On their own (and even together), I'm not sure these answers are satisfactory. I struggle to take solace in them, especially when it comes to the deaths of innocent children or helpless people falling victim to genocide all across the world. So allow me to provide another answer. Like those listed before, it may not be complete, but it does provide me some comfort and maybe it will provide you comfort as well.

Think of a treasured memory from childhood. It can be small, so long as it's meaningful. Here's the example I'll use: being a small child and roaming the neighborhood with friends and family on Halloween, trick or treating, and having fun. There's nothing particularly special about this memory, but despite being simple, it's joyous. I can look back and feel the happi-ness I felt back then in full, vivid detail despite many years having passed.

Now, think of a memory of a loved one you've lost. I remember being young and sitting side by side with my Grandfather while we watched science-fiction movies at his house. We wouldn't talk much, and what we watched wasn't anything relevant enough to mention, but it was a bonding experience I look back on fondly. I felt safe by my Grandfather's side. I felt loved and appreciated. And, I felt like he was welcoming me into a new, exciting world full of spaceships, aliens, and adventure. Some years after this memory (really, it's a collection of similar memories), my Grandfather passed away — and that was a very long time ago.

Yet, despite all the time that's passed, I can sit here and re-experience my memories of my Grandfather. I can feel what I felt then in full color and texture. All the love and security he offered shines as brightly now as it did back then. That's no small thing.

Everything that exists exists forever in time. Though we appear to leave experiences in the past, they don't actually go anywhere. My experience of trick or treating exists. Not only does it exist, it exists presently, as evidenced by my being able to experience it here and now. Same with my memories of my Grandfather.

All too often, when an experience comes to an end (whether that be the sun setting on a beautiful beach vacation or a loved one passing away), we mourn the loss of something we've never experienced. We mourn our never experiencing all the future days spent on the beach now that vacation is over. We mourn the days and weeks and years we were meant to spend with our loved one that now we'll never be able to. This is a natural process. When something that's been a big part of your life goes away, a mourning process will ensue. Even saints weep over the deaths of those they love.

But, despite our mourning, it's important to remember that in life being lost, beauty can be found. A child who dies of cancer — courageous and full of life all the way to the end — leaves a mark on eternity. Their innocence and strength in a time of grave illness resonates out through time and space. They become a beacon of courage that anyone can access at any time. Those who suffered and died in the Holocaust — they, too, become beacons. Beacons of love, bravery, and strength. We often hear about survivors of the concentration camps because of the triumph of their spirit. But even those who were lost didn't suffer in vain. When we hear about their plight almost a century later, we're driven to states of deep emotion because they are beacons of justice — despite all the injustices imposed on them. Their light shines so brightly that the world is a markedly more just place now than it was in the 1940s.

The purpose of acknowledging this is not to deny others the suffering they've experienced. Nor is it to selfishly reap the rewards of their strength and love. I am not suggesting that some people have to die unfairly so as to set a good example for the rest of us.

But what I am saying is this — don't let the pain of loss cloud the beauty of existence. It is not "fair" that some die young while others do not. It is not "fair" that some suffer while others inflict suffering. But I'm not sure this is a game of "fair" vs. "unfair." There's immense beauty in the world, even in loss. It'd be a shame not to let the love and courage of the child who has died shine brightly down upon us because we're lost in our mourning. We can mourn and still let the beauty of what people and things were when they were here shine.

Whether you're of a Christian faith or not, it's undeniable that hundreds of millions of people find strength through Christ. In times of hardship, they call upon him, and his memory gives them the strength to overcome. Would that be the case had Jesus not died on the cross? Would he be a beacon of unconditional love, forgiveness, and hope? No. Christ needed to die in order to be reborn. In order to inspire in others, thousands of miles away and thousands of years in the future, the hope that life is eternal. What we admire most about every beloved religious figure is not so much what they did but the context in which they did it. These people are icons not only because they were kind and loving but because they were kind and loving in a time and place where it would've been very easy to be cruel and dejected.

As I stated at the start of this chapter, this answer isn't intended to be fully explanatory. But some of the most powerful forces of love, kindness, and strength in the world were born long ago in instances of loss and suffering, and I want to make sure we don't overlook that.

CHAPTER THIRTY

Religious Backlash Against Mysticism, Sorcery, and General Occultism

If you were raised in any of the three major Abrahamic religious traditions, you're probably aware that there's a general aversion to all practices deemed "magical," "mystical," or "occult." The teachings outlined in this book could be considered (if one were inclined to consider them so) as falling into all three categories. Personally, I wouldn't consider them any of the above, but in the grand scheme of things, what I consider them is meaningless. You consider them whatever you want. And know that some will consider them sacrilegious and evil.

At least in Christian traditions (particularly Catholicism, the tradition in which I was raised and am most familiar), all things even slightly "mystical" are considered sinful. So sinful, in fact, that for a large portion of the last 1500 years, people were jailed, tortured, and killed for having been labeled "mystics" or "sorcerers." As with many things, I think the general Christian position against mysticism and magic started out with good intentions, then slowly degenerated into something ridiculous and persecutory over time. And now there are a lot of misconceptions floating around. So, I'd like to try and clear some of them up.

Conscious creation is neither evil nor sinful by its nature. Everyone is "creating" all the time. To become aware of what you're creating and to make adjustments to your inner state based on that awareness doesn't suddenly mean you're an evil wizard who'll burn in hell for eternity. On a busy highway, every car is traveling at a certain speed. Some people are checking their speedometer, some aren't — but everyone is moving along just the same. By checking your speed, you give yourself a means by which you can adjust your speed. Your awareness of how fast you are going makes you less likely to speed, less likely to cause an accident, and all around less likely to create any harm or chaos.

Think of conscious creation as a spiritual speed check. Its purpose is to give you more agency in your life. By seeing how you've been creating in the past, you can make adjustments to your behavior that have a positive impact on your life and the world at large. To suggest that one's knowledge of the power to create his own reality makes them more likely to act with malicious intentions is ignorant at best and the most dangerous form of fear-mongering at worst.

Do some people try to use their knowledge of manifestation to hurt others and sow negativity in the world? Sure — in the exact way that some people check their speedometer, see they're over the speed limit, and choose to accelerate anyway. But these people are in the minority, and without exception, they're people who have a very tenuous grasp of the teachings to begin with. If you've taken anything from this book so far, it should be that the inner states you hold manifest in your external experience. So if you were to try and manifest something negative happening to another person, by definition, you'd be forced to hold a negative internal state, and would be bringing a whole host of awful manifestations unto yourself, too. In short, if you were to read this book and think for a second about trying to create an outcome based on feelings of malice, you'd have not understood almost anything that's been discussed (and you'd likely ruin your own life before you could manage to manifest anything productively negative in the lives of others).

As I mentioned, I think the advisory against "sorcery" in so many spiritual traditions was genuinely well-intentioned at some point. To grasp at happiness in objects and events outside of yourself is an exercise in futility. You won't find happiness in this, that, or anywhere "over there." Happiness is right here — you are happiness, and the more clearly you see that, the more your external world will come to reflect peace, love, and joy. The urge of many teachers throughout history to dismiss the practice of conscious creation was likely based on this intuition. And when you're preaching to the masses, trying to lead them toward spiritual salvation, it can sometimes be better not to venture into the gray areas — the places where information could be misunderstood or mis-implemented to the detriment of whoever fails to understand the finer points of what you're teaching.

But in my eyes, the reward of properly understanding the mechanisms of conscious creation far outweigh the risks. When you understand things clearly, you'll see that manifestation is compatible with lots of traditional religious beliefs and is in no way a force of evil. And if you don't trust me, maybe you'll trust Jesus:

"And so I tell you, keep on asking, and you will receive what you ask for. Keep on seeking, and you will find. Keep on knocking, and the door will be opened to you. For everyone who asks, receives. Everyone who seeks, finds. And to everyone who knocks, the door will be opened." Luke 11:9-10.

"Whatever you ask for in prayer, believe that you have received it, and it will be yours. And when you stand praying, if you hold anything against anyone, forgive them, so that your Father in heaven may forgive you your sins." Mark 11:24-25

Or the prophet Muhammad:

"Actions only go by intentions. Everyone gets what they intend."

"Surely Allah does not change the conditions in which a people are in until they change that which is in themselves."

Or the Buddha:

"All that we are is the result of what we have thought."

"What you are is what you have been. What you'll be is what you do now."

"All experiences are preceded by mind, having mind as their master, created by mind."

You get the point. And if you go looking, you'll find countless more examples of revered spiritual masters speaking similarly. Conscious creation is at the heart of every major religious tradition, and you shouldn't fear it or believe that it's wrong because someone who doesn't understand their own faith told you so.

Section V:
Dialogues

Learning Via Conversation

Very often, we learn best through discussion and dialogue. It's one thing to take on ideas in essay form — it's a great thing, actually — but still, there is value in having our questions answered directly. Because the nature of the written medium is for information to travel in one direction, from writer to reader, we don't have the luxury of talking one-on-one. But, I have had discussions with hundreds of people over the years, and have kept records of those conversations.

In the following pages, I'll include the questions I think are most pertinent and will prove most useful. Maybe something that's been bothering you will be answered there. Or, even better, maybe someone else's mind will have gone in a direction yours never would've, but nevertheless, that illuminates everything for you. Note that these dialogues are in question-answer format and come from discussions with many different people.

How are we able to change into a desired state? Are you suggesting that we just commit entirely to the desired state in our mind simply by stating that we are what we want to be?

More so, what I'm saying is there's no need to change states. When a desire arises, we experience it first and foremost as the knowing of having the desired object/experience.

If I want to vacation in Spain, the desire blooms as the knowing of being on a Spanish beach. It's only after I know this that I impose the additional thought/feeling, "But how will I afford that?" or "I can't take that many days off work," or whatever. This is an unnecessary imposition. It's just a way you create an imaginary distance between yourself and the desired state.

So my point is, that to even feel an urge to "change" states is a misunderstanding. You don't need to change your state; you need to see clearly that you were in your desired state the second the desire arose, but you turned away from it and can easily make a decision to stop turning away in the future.

Let your desires bloom fully as the knowing of the experience you seek to manifest — then stop there. This is why Neville Goddard cautions against worrying about the "how" and the "why" because the second you start doing that, you've ceased to know the desired state, and instead, you've chosen to know yourself as someone who needs to take action to access that state.

What you are suggesting is, if I understand correctly, to just accept the arising desire as already being the state and stop right there. To not think about how it's going to happen. It seems like that's very hard for most people to do.

Yes. It is hard for most people to do. But it's hard because of a primary misunderstanding — that I am a separate person who exists at the center of all my different thoughts and feelings.

When you investigate that separate self — when you stop taking it for granted that you are the person in the center of everything — and see that you are nothing more than your knowing at this very moment, it should click why I'm saying it's actually very easy to hold the state of your desire.

I don't agree with — or perhaps understand — your assertion that we can't desire something without first knowing what it feels like to have it. That's not my lived experience, and I'm lost as to why you would say it with such certainty. As a young boy, I remember wanting to kiss a girl for the first time; I had zero idea or "knowing" what it would be like — the excitement, the warmth, the flood of emotions, the awkwardness afterward, etc. So please explain what you mean. If one has never had an comparable experience, they just can't know what it would feel like. They can create an imaginary approximation/version of what something might feel like (maybe that's what you mean), but that's a huge discrepancy.

Here is what I mean: When you desire something, you desire it because of the state or feeling that thing represents to you. When you desire to kiss a girl, there must be a reason you have that desire, right? You don't desire it blindly. Of course not; there is a state you'd like to experience — again, there must be, which is why I say it with such certainty.

Now, whether the state you experience when actually kissing a girl (or the specific thoughts/sensations/perceptions) is the same as the state you were seeking to experience when your desire was born is a different story.

Remember, we're manifesting all the time, so few experiences exist in isolation. The experience of kissing a girl might be a manifestation of your desire to be in a state of love and connection, but also of your knowing of awkwardness, or embarrassment, or whatever.

It's also worth noting that the more adept you become at manifestation, the more closely your manifested experiences will come to resemble the initial state you desired. When you aren't working consciously, you'll always have to contend with every aspect of knowing that you hold with any regularity. When you are more intentional with your states of knowing, they will manifest more directly, unaffected by tons of other states.

In practical terms (if I understand correctly), it is not necessary to know exactly how flying a fighter jet would feel, so long as we have a clear idea of the experience we're seeking. To out-picture this experience in 3D reality, must we assume the state of already having flown the jet? Should we feel the same way about having flown the jet as we feel about having put on our socks this morning? How do you assume the state of a "fighter jet pilot" if you haven't experienced it yet? And does the state of being a fighter jet pilot include all other aspects of your personality mixed together, or is it a singular, distinct state?

Flying a fighter jet isn't any objective state in and of itself. For you, flying a fighter jet might be a state of exhilaration, excitement, and joy. For me, it might be a state of terror and anxiety.

How we represent different "states" or "knowings" to ourselves is irrelevant. Different things represent different states to different people.

What matters is you hold the state that your specific desire is representative of to you. Maybe you don't know what it's literally like to fly a fighter jet, but if the reason you want to fly one is because of all the awesome feelings you feel when you imagine it, then live in the knowing of those feelings and it'll manifest.

Do you recommend imagining scenes and feelings that might occur *after* the desire has come pass? For example, rather than imagining flying a jet, you might imagine a friend sending you a message saying, "Dude, just saw the video of you flying a jet!"

Let your desires guide you. Once you're in the right place of understanding, there's no need to cajole or manipulate your desires in order to make them manifest.

A knowing of some state will simply arise in the form of a desire, and you'll allow yourself to rest in that knowing — then it'll manifest. So, if what you desire to know is the exhilaration of flying a jet, live in that knowing. If what you desire to know is the adulation of your friends for having flown a fighter jet, live in that knowing.

What is the difference between fantasy and knowing your desire fulfilled? Aren't they kind of the same thing?

Imagine a kid the night before Christmas. She might be up all night, tossing and turning, bursting with excitement over all the gifts that will be under the tree the next morning. Is this a fantasy? Maybe you'd say it is. But it's a fantasy with a level of certainty underlying it. Christmas Day will come. There's no doubt about it. There will be gifts under the tree — etc., etc.

That type of fantasy is different from someone who is a terrible singer fantasizing about being a pop star. You might bask in the imagined experience of being on stage singing and dancing for thousands of screaming fans, but on some level, you know it's just a fantasy. At your core, you "know" you're getting high on the emotions of the fantasy — you don't actually believe it's a situation that's going to occur.

Obviously, the bad singer could manifest singing ability and thus become a pop star one day, but you get the point.

So, basically, the difference is one is more easily believable than the other. In other words, one is a fantasy and the other an expectation. Do you mean to say we must only dwell on what we expect or what we fantasize must become what we expect?

I'd argue it goes beyond belief. Do you believe the sun is going to set tonight, then rise tomorrow? Or is that a fact so concrete it transcends belief?

Put another way, you know your name. You don't believe you know it; you just know it. We should strive to "know" the feeling of having what we want to manifest now, not believe we'll get it someday.

If I was born into a poor family, how can I access the sensation of being rich?

Imagine waking up in a mansion, sitting by your awesome pool, driving your expensive car, etc.

I like the expression, "The map is not the territory." It serves to remind us that the map we hold in our hands is not literally the same thing as the territory it references, but is a representation of that territory. Our desires are no different. Your desire to be rich is not a desire for a mansion, a pool, or a fancy car. Your desire is to feel rich. Maybe this feels like security, abundance, comfort, or whatever — but the mansion, the pool, and the fancy car are just ways you represent the desired feeling to yourself. The objects you desire are the map and the feelings you desire are the territory.

So I say, it doesn't matter whether you've never been rich. It doesn't matter if you've never woken up in a mansion, sat by your pool, or driven a fancy car. You can still access how it'd feel to be rich. You are accessing that feeling anytime the desire arises. Live there.

How far do we have to dig to discover what our feeling truly is? In this example, she wants to be rich. But the desire to be rich is not just a desire for a mansion, pool, car, etc. — but for feelings of security and abundance. Do we need to go further and look inside as to why these feelings of security and abundance are important to us? Or just live in the original level of feelings?

That's a fantastic question. The answer is yes. The answer is also no. The answer is also, it depends.

For the purpose of manifestation, no, you don't have to dig any deeper than the initial level of feeling or knowing. There's a caveat to that, though. Sometimes, our desire for certain feelings or states can be rooted in deep emotional issues. Someone who grew up in an insecure environment might be obsessed with making money because they're obsessed with security — they never feel safe, they always feel like they're going to lose the roof over their head. In most cases, even this won't be an impediment, as holding the feeling of the thing you desire is enough to overcome insecurity. But I have worked with people who were so deeply scarred that their insecurities seemed to sneak up in strange ways. So, in those cases, it depends.

When it comes to the things you manifest making you feel fulfilled? The answer is absolutely, no doubt about it, 100% yes. That's a whole spiritual journey in and of itself, though. No need to worry about it until you've mastered manifestation. As wealthy people are so fond of saying, "Money can't buy happiness." And that's true, but I think everyone should get money first, then face that fact second.

A lot of people ask questions about manifesting new relationships. What do you do when you're already in a relationship, but it's going poorly?

Oftentimes, when we're unhappy with our partner (whether that be a specific behavior of theirs or just in a general sense), it's because we've come to rely on/expect them to make us feel a certain way. This is totally natural. But, as with most things, just because it's natural doesn't mean it isn't worth investigating.

To love is the most selfless act possible. Love is, in fact, what we are — what we're made of. Lester Levenson put it this way: "To love is to accept someone completely, just as they are." And this acceptance isn't a worldly acceptance — don't mistake it for approval. It's a very passive allowance. An allowing of the other person to shine exactly as they are. I often think of the love a Mother has for her child. The baby doesn't have to do anything to earn love. The Mother loves him/her on the very basis of his/her existence. No judgment, no expectation of receiving anything in return for one's love. It's a state bordering on awe.

Anything less than this is not love. To expect something in return for one's "love" is just dependence masquerading as love. And most "relationships" are exactly that — a mutual dependence masquerading as love. It's why so many relationships fail. I expect you to be the way you used to be, or the way I thought you'd turn out, or the way I am now, even if I was different in the past — and you expect the same from me.

The solution is to get back to love. A complete, open acceptance. And on some level, most people (even those struggling in their current relationship) are in touch with this.

It can sound like a tall order to accept so wholly, especially when the person in question has come to annoy or frustrate you. Actually, it's easy. To love is the easiest thing any of us can ever do — because it requires no effort; it's just allowing.

And here's the best part about it. People tend to soften when exposed to this kind of love. Actually, they tend to melt. It's like Ali v. Foreman and the rope-a-dope — when you meet someone at acceptance and love, they might still lash out and do mean or dismissive things at first, but quickly, they'll punch themselves out. At that point, two people come together again and the flame burns brightly as ever.

What is the thing I must face? I don't get it — If I feel undeserving on some level, how am I supposed to face love when I feel I don't deserve it?

If you feel undeserving of love, let that feeling take center stage for a while. And make sure that's the deepest level of it. The mind is clever — people will get close to facing the thing they don't want to but subtly soften the blow right when they get too near. For example, someone might say, "I don't deserve love because I'm a jerk who hurts people." On some level, that might be true, but the real issue is likely "I'm afraid that no matter what I do, nobody will love me." In this case, you feel inherently undeserving of love, as opposed to undeserving because of some controllable action. A person who is a jerk and hurts the people close to them usually does so as a subconscious defense mechanism to that second fear I mentioned. Basically, at a subconscious level, they're saying, "I'm going to be a jerk and hurt people because then I'll have a good explanation for why I feel unloved, and don't have to face that fear that maybe no matter what I do I won't be loved."

So, to get back on point, try and trace down to the deepest level of the negative feeling. Then, face it fully. Let it expand and grow as much as you need to. You might shake. You might cry. You might feel as terrible as you've ever felt before. But if you don't fight it and don't try to explain it to yourself, the feeling will eventually run its course. Then, it'll be gone and you'll feel a whole lot better — like a weight has been lifted off your shoulders.

It's counterintuitive, but we don't have to "do" anything to change these deeply held negative feelings. They only have a strong impact when we hide from them. Think of it like springs that you're stuffing down inside of yourself. When you stop pushing down on them and let them do what they want to do, they'll spring up and out of you. When they do, you'll have a whole lot more energy because you'll no longer need every bit of strength to keep the springs from popping up into your mind.

How do I trace it down? Should I do some kind of visualization? Maybe imagine a dark cloud taking over my body and destroying it?

I don't know if a visualization is necessary. I do know that some people do exercises like that. Except, instead of imagining the black fog destroying you, they'd say to imagine the black fog flowing out of you — remember, ultimately what we're seeking to do is uncover these negative feelings so we can let them go. It may feel bad, in the way that a splinter feels worse while you're removing it than it does when you just let it be there. But like a splinter, by going through the uncomfortable removal process we end up freeing ourselves from the dull, quiet pain of letting it stay where it is. Don't actively try to make yourself feel worse or ruminate on negative things in a way that makes you feel hopeless. It's an exploration, not a torture test.

You could also just quiet your mind, with the intention of facing whatever it is you need to face, then wait for thoughts to come up. If you don't interfere with the thoughts as they arise, it probably won't be long before you feel the deeper, more painful thoughts start rearing their heads.

That's why I use the analogy of a spring. These negative thoughts tend to be "pressurized" to some degree. We use a lot of energy to keep them stuffed down inside. Some people overthink, some people overeat, some people overdrink — all that stuff is a means of holding down what we don't want to face. So, when you clear your head and allow the negative feelings to rise up, they tend to pop up quite easily, like a spring "springing up" when you stop pushing down on it.

What is a state? Are states temporary feelings like being happy because of great news, then feeling awful because of bad news?

A "state" can be a combination of emotions, not just one emotion in isolation. it's kind of like an entire symphony vs. a single instrument.

Imagine walking into an exam. In scenario 1, you didn't prepare at all. You walk in feeling anxious, upset, stupid, etc. In addition to those feelings, there's likely a "knowing" that you're not going to do very well. Or, at minimum, a knowing that it's very likely you won't do well. We can class all these things together and call them "state 1."

In scenario 2, you had been studying for weeks leading up to the exam. You walk in feeling cool, calm, collected, intelligent, and you have a "knowing" that you're likely going to do great. Again, let's put all these small things together and Label them "state 2."

Even though in both situations you are taking the same action (walking into the exam), you're doing so in very different "states."

In our lives, generally, we're always in some "state" — there's always some combination of feeling and knowing going on in our experience, even if the feelings aren't particularly intense. Many people get stuck in increasingly negative states over time — this leads to unhappiness. In order to manifest what you want, you must take on the "state" that you'd be in if you had the thing you're trying to manifest.

This is getting clearer now. So, how do I induce feelings that correspond with my wish being fulfilled? Is it just assuming something is the case? Like a sort of delusion?

Personally, I don't like the term delusion. Some people love it, and it works for them, but for me, it just doesn't sit right.

Here's an example I've used in the past. Say I want to take a vacation to Spain. That desire arises first as the "knowing" of myself on a Spanish beach. In fact, it's only because this knowing arises that I desire to take the trip — it arises and I enjoy the feeling/state/knowing of being on the beach.

But then, I put an imaginary distance between myself and this knowing. I say, "I don't have the money to go to Spain," or "I can't take a week off work." Then, I start doing exercises to try and re-access the state or knowing of being in Spain. But that's an incredible over-complication. You don't have to do anything to access the knowing of your desire fulfilled. When your desire arose in the first place, it arose as that knowing. You have to *not do* what everyone does and place an imaginary distance between yourself and that state.

This could also be thought of as basking in the pleasant part of your desire. The part that makes you desire a trip to Spain, or a loving relationship, or a well-paying job. If you stay in the pleasant part and drop the "lack-centric" part (the part where you feel bad because you don't have what you desire), then your desire will manifest.

While facing our inner demons, we have to feel deep-seated emotions. I am scared that this can also trigger manifestations. What if I manifest more of the bad feeling or emotion? How can I release without that happening?

It's natural to feel that way. In fact, that's the exact reason why people refuse to look at their uncomfortable feelings. They're afraid if I look under my bed, the monster is going to attack me. But by not looking at your demons, you're allowing them to live rent-free in your subconscious 24 hours a day, 7 days a week.

If you don't acknowledge your demons, they'll make you acknowledge them — by manifesting in your life. There's no running away, no hiding. You have to face up.

Do you do anything beyond examining the painful belief to release it? Are there any questions to ask yourself that help with releasing? I am concerned I might be able to find the painful beliefs, but that I'll just sit with them and feel them but not be able to do enough to heal them. Is feeling them all that is needed?

It can be helpful to contextualize them a bit. Here's what I mean. You might have this deep "feeling" that you're a loser. You may sit with it for a while and struggle to release. In that situation, it might be helpful to trace it back. You'll often stumble on some forgotten memory that is the root cause of that feeling. "I feel like a loser because in third grade, Joe Smith told me I'm a loser for liking Pokemon instead of Dragon Ball Z." Sometimes, when we get to the first instance of a feeling, it hits a lot harder than the dull pain it has turned into over time. And then you realize your entire life has been colored by an off-handed comment made to you by another 8-year-old, and it's much easier to release.

I'm not afraid to face my fears or my feelings, but I still can't manifest what I want. I'm not sure what the hang-up is at this point or how to find out. It's incredibly frustrating.

Let your frustration guide you. One of the things Lester was fond of saying was, "If you get stuck while releasing, release the feeling of stuck-ness."

Basically, if you feel frustrated and like you're doing the work but not seeing the benefits, investigate why. Personally, I had to release a lot of fears in the ballpark of "this is never going to work," "There are no answers out there," and, "I'm destined to feel stuck and miserable for the rest of my life."

Before I faced them, these feelings manifested as bashing my head against the wall but never making any progress or coming to new levels of understanding, even though I was putting massive amounts of effort in — and was more than willing (or so I thought) to face what needed to be faced.

I have been dealing with obsessive intrusive thoughts for a while, and they are incredibly active when I try to be aware and live in the moment. They are mainly fears about what could go wrong with my loved ones. When I faced them directly and asked

why they never leave me alone, they answered something like this: I want to protect you. I don't want you to suffer.

I also realized that I am worried about other's safety because if something happens, there would be no one to love me back.

These feelings always find their way back to me. What do you think I should do?

That's a common issue. One I struggled with and one I think everyone struggles with to some degree. Start by having no agenda with your feelings — don't allow them up just so you can tell them to sit down or try to talk them out of terrorizing you. Just let them be. To let something be without interfering or wanting to change it is the true meaning of love. That's divine love. "Human love" is something more like approval. So you don't have to approve of the part of yourself that is afraid; just allow it to be what it is.

Your intuition is correct. Your fears and feelings do exist to protect you. But, like an overbearing mother, in an attempt to shield you from pain, they end up causing you pain.

It's almost as if your mind goes, "So that I don't feel the pain of losing a loved one later, I'm going to simulate the pain of losing them now — by doing this, I'll remain vigilant in protecting my loved ones, and thus not have to feel the pain of losing them in the future."

The truth is this: In life, we will lose loved ones. We can live in simulated pain and anxiety all we want in an attempt to protect the people we love, but ultimately, we will lose them anyway. And when we do, the pain at that moment will not be any less for our having spent years living in pain. So, our "protection mechanism" is a faulty one. It doesn't lessen the pain of loss and clouds over our happiness with extra, unnecessary pain.

It's normal to fear loss because we vest our happiness in people and things outside of ourselves. Exactly as you said, it's ultimately an issue of self-love — we give over parts of ourselves to other people and things, so to lose them is also to lose a part of ourselves. But it doesn't have to be this way.

Think of a great memory from your life. From my own life, I'll use the example of being a small child and trick-or-treating with friends on Halloween. I'm not upset because this event has come and gone. I look back on it fondly. If anything, I look at it more fondly today than I did at the moment. The "love" I felt in that moment is stronger now than ever. This is the case because I haven't invested any part of myself in that memory. I don't feel part of me is lost because it's come and gone.

Our relationship with loved ones is no different. When they go, expectedly or by surprise, our lives will change. Inevitably, there will be a mourning process. But, our love for them will never diminish. Like the memory of playing with friends, we'll look back on it and smile — the love will grow stronger even though the moment has come and gone.

I have this defense mechanism of trying very hard to dig up and feel/allow/release these negative feelings. How do I move past this? Also, sometimes when I release, I feel a bit of relief, but the negative emotion is still there — especially for big issues. Do I have to release everything in one go?

Try not to be forceful. Remember, releasing is an "allowing" process. You don't want to have an agenda with your feelings — you don't want to approach them with a sense of urgency, desperate to get rid of them. Let them come up on their terms. It won't take long if you don't resist.

I would say you don't have to actively "dig" negative thoughts or feelings up. Sit quietly, clear your mind, and wait. Or, think about what you want to manifest, but keep your ear pressed to the door to see if any negative feelings come knocking. If nothing pops up, then nothing is blocking you. You can be doing this all day — stay very attuned to when negative feelings come around so you can try and release them instead of shoving them back inside. But if a tree falls in the forest and nobody is around to hear it, then who cares if it makes a sound — you'll know if a feeling is blocking you.

As for the big issues not resolving completely, again, don't put pressure on yourself. Release at the pace you feel comfortable. There's no right or wrong in this — if you can release everything at once, awesome. But, if your body/mind rejects an attempt to do that, start smaller and come back to the big stuff later.

What are your thoughts on taking action or looking in the world for progress being made toward your manifestation? Every few weeks, I "check-in" to assess what progress has been made so that I can readjust my process if the thing I want to manifest is not coming closer — then I go back to living in the end of my desire fulfilled. Will this kind of checking hinder my progress?

This is a good question — and one that requires some nuance to answer.

On the one hand, a lack of progress or movement in the world could be an indication you need to tweak the way you're approaching what you want to manifest. Let's use something banal as an example: If I was expecting a package on Monday, and now it's Friday, and I still haven't received my stuff — not even an update — that's an indication something is wrong. Maybe I typed my address incorrectly, or maybe my package was lost/destroyed. But I need to look into what the issue may be. So, lack of progress toward your desires could mean you "typed the address wrong," metaphorically speaking.

On the other hand, we have to be careful about the motivation for our checking in. If sunrise is supposed to be at 6:30 tomorrow and at 7:15 it's still pretty dark outside, you wouldn't think anything of it. Maybe it's foggy, maybe it's raining — but the sun didn't explode, and you'd never feel compelled to check in and see if it did. We don't check in on things we know are going to happen, even if they're a little behind schedule in their development.

You have to judge your check-ins on a case by case basis. If you feel compelled to check in regularly, it might be because you don't actually believe your desire is on the way — kind of like texting your crush, then checking your phone every 30 seconds for the next 5 hours. With each passing minute, you get more and more worried; you sink deeper and deeper into a "knowing" that he/she isn't going to text you back. But, at the same time, if something just strikes you as off about no movement having occurred, then I don't think it's inherently bad to check-in. Again — if I know my package should be here on Monday, I don't think much of it on Tuesday (it probably got delayed), but by Friday, it's obvious I need to investigate.

I'm trying to manifest a relationship with a specific person. As I begin to see that she is not reacting to my expectations, negative feelings arise. If I release the root cause of these negative feelings, it amounts to mourning this hypothetical relationship. How is it possible to manifest this relationship if I actually mourn it?

Releasing shouldn't amount to mourning. Mourning necessitates the presence of negative feelings — by definition, it's a state of "I want but don't have," or "I want but will never have", and the not having-ness makes us feel as if we lack.

What you should be trying to release are the root feelings that make you feel a sense of lack for not having the relationship. Why do you feel as if something is lost by not being with this person? Do you feel like you're unworthy if they don't want to be with you? What is it you want from them? Why do you feel the relationship needs to be two-directional (I give you love and you give me love), and don't feel satisfied through loving them alone?

I'm not specifically asking you these questions or trying to see what your answer is. I'm just trying to clarify the types of questions we should be asking ourselves. When you release these deeper feelings, there won't be a sense of mourning.

What do you mean when you say an emotion can be a defense mechanism?

Here's an example: Say I am up for a promotion at work but feel as if I won't get it based on my belief that office politics are too important, and that that's an area I struggle in. Every time I see my boss laughing with my coworkers, it makes me angry — "This is just a popularity contest, making the boss laugh shouldn't be a criteria for promotion."

That type of belief is always a defense mechanism. What it's defending against might differ from person to person, though. Maybe I have a belief that I'm not good at my job, and my hatred of office politics is stopping me from looking at that. You see this all the time all over the world. People complain about how unfair things are and how he didn't deserve this, or she only got that because she's pretty, etc.

Maybe my deeper feeling is more general — that I don't have what it takes to be successful. In that case, my lack of likability or political aptitude becomes a convenient excuse. It allows me to play the victim and act as if the reason I'm not getting what I want is out of my control. People will go to hell and back defending their view that the world is not fair or that people are rewarded undeservedly in situations where they deserved success. A deeper feeling of inadequacy always underlies these belief. Always.

When someone gets chosen for the promotion over you, it stings because, for the slightest moment, you're faced with the thought, "This person is better than me." When you're a musician and some other band gets the record deal, you might angrily say, "They suck. People don't understand what good music is. This whole industry is bull-shit." What's really going on is, you feel like (you don't even need to think it consciously because it happens so fast, though, I will be verbalizing the feeling), "Wait a second. They think that band is better than mine? Are they right? Do I stink?" But that's not something you want to face, so you get to rationalizing.

I have a deep -seated belief that the entire world is against me. I can't seem to find any other belief that underlies it. What can I do?

The "world is against me" belief is a very common emotional defense mechanism. So you're not alone in feeling this way. But, my advice is to ask what purpose this belief serves. Is the world being against you a way to hide from feelings that maybe you're just not good enough? When you sit down to do your creative work, are you nagged by a feeling that your project is going to suck, and you really don't want to face that feeling?

If you want more extensive advice on this specific question, *Letting Go* by David Hawkins is a book I'd recommend. He talks about the "me vs. World" perspective extensively and offers advice on how to rise above it. But my answer is just that this belief must serve a purpose to you — it must be guarding your conscious mind from getting too close to some deeper subconscious fear or negative belief, even if you can't see it yet.

How do you feel the feelings you need to without identifying with them? What is the difference between entertaining a thought and creating more and releasing?

When we "entertain" thoughts, we're very rarely making direct contact with our limiting feelings. We're dealing with our painful reactions to those feelings — reactions our subconscious mind sets up precisely to prevent us from facing the deeper thought or belief. When people spiral into negative thinking/feeling, this is usually what's happening. They're ruminating on their reactions.

Here's an example. Say a person is insecure about their weight. Every time they look in the mirror, they feel bad. Every outfit they try on makes them feel heavy. They try to cultivate self-love, but keep ending up in spirals of self-hatred. In a case like this, the person should try and find out what underlies their physical insecurity. Treat your negative thoughts or beliefs as reactions, not as the core problematic feelings. So that person might ask, what purpose does my insecurity about my weight serve? Do I feel deep down that nobody will ever love me, and my body becomes a lightning rod for that? As in, do I feel inherently unlovable and prevent myself from facing that by saying, "I am unlovable because of my weight." This is the exact reason so many people struggle with changing their physical bodies. Because their physical bodies are expressions of deeper feelings they don't want to face. If that person doesn't address their feeling inherently unlovable, they won't be able to change their body.

That person might also ask, why am I carrying extra weight in the first place? Is that in and of itself a defense mechanism? In many cases, victims of sexual trauma in youth struggle with obesity later in life. Extra weight becomes a defense mechanism. Because there is a cultural stigma that obesity is unattractive, someone who feels it is dangerous to be attractive (because of their being preyed upon at an earlier time) may subconsciously create a body that they deem unattractive so as to not be hurt again. Again, I use the body example just because it can be helpful for seeing the types of questions we have to ask ourselves. When you hit the root feeling, it's generally neutral. It isn't painful in and of itself; our resistance to it is painful. And when we entertain negativity, it's not because we're entertaining our true feelings; it's because we're stuck entertaining our intentionally painful defense mechanisms that are designed to make us uncomfortable so we never address the deeper issue.

My discovery of "manifestation" has led to a diminishment of my mental health. I feel as if I've learned some new information that I can't forget but that I'll never be able to use effectively to improve my life. In fact, I now feel as if my anxiety and fear are going to lead to more intense manifestations of things I don't want to happen.

It can be incredibly difficult when our knowledge of manifestation gets hijacked and becomes a manifestation of our deeper struggles and mental health issues. If it's any reassurance, you won't manifest negativity for anyone in your life. The insidious thing about anxiety is that it tends to lead to manifestations which make us more fearful, but that are ultimately benign. They breed more anxiety — when something bad actually happens, the anxiety is neutralized. So don't worry about accidentally manifesting something negative. It won't happen.

Further, try and see how your current feeling is just a manifestation of deeper issues that have been there since way before you knew about all this stuff. When we start to go inward, our struggles get closer to consciousness, and thus, they seem to be more prominent. It can feel like we're moving backward, when really we're moving forwards by getting closer to uncovering the things that've been holding us back. Knowledge of conscious creation isn't Pandora's box — it's not like by learning about it, you've crossed a border from whence you can't return and are now in a race against the clock to figure out how to do it correctly before you mess something up. If you never thought about manifestation again, your life would proceed perfectly fine. Some good things would happen, some bad, and you'd have full power to act in the world as you would've before in order to improve things. This knowledge can only ever make your life better, never worse. Again, it can feel worse because you're getting closer to internalized issues, but that's just an illusion. Try not to stress; just see that you're playing with house money now. All that can happen is you can win.

In terms of general mental health, I always advise the basics. Eat well, exercise, meditate, and consider therapy. If you're struggling, don't hesitate to contact a mental health professional. People often feel like this isn't the "spiritual route," but personally, I think the progress made with a professional is a manifestation of the hope and determination that things can improve. So I always recommend it.

Is the releasing process supposed to feel like a forgetting of the problem? When I release, how can I know that I'm actually releasing the feeling/belief completely rather than letting it return to the subconscious mind? For example, I'm trying to release the deep feelings of being unlovable and inferior. Sometimes, even after I note these feelings and decide to release them, they disappear for a while and I feel fine — but then they reappear later (on rare occasions, even with greater intensity). I'm not sure if that's normal and I just need to keep on releasing, or if perhaps I am accidentally suppressing and/or intensifying those feelings? Also, do you think that consciously deciding to release the feel-

ing/belief is something I should avoid doing because it should happen naturally?

In my experience, releasing isn't so much of a forgetting as it is a feeling of resolution. When a painful emotion just kind of drifts out of mind, it'll often come back again as it hasn't actually been resolved. When the problematic emotion has been seen clearly and released, there should be a noticeable sense of relief. All the sting comes out of the thought or memory, and you know without a doubt that it isn't a problem anymore.

I want to emphasize again that this is a process of clear seeing. You don't have to hope something has been released. The release will come spontaneously when you've faced the truth of how you feel. If the release doesn't come, then dig deeper. And I don't think there's a problem with consciously making a decision to release if that helps you.

You once said that the core feeling you have to release won't be something you feel negatively about. If I feel negativity around the feeling of being unlovable or inferior, does that mean I'm not at the core yet?

When we get down close to the core issue or emotion, there's a very fine line between our problematic feelings and our reactions to those feelings. I tend to believe that if you're experiencing something painful or unpleasant, you're at the level of reaction — maybe an incredibly subtle reaction that's almost indiscernible from the root issue, but a reaction nevertheless. I can't say for certain that this is the case in 100% of situations, but it has been my experience. And don't let what I'm saying confuse or inspire stress in you — I'm not saying you're blind to what the real issue is and have to go on this wild investigation to find out what your true problem is. All I'd suggest is you see if you're actually facing your feeling of being unloved and inferior or if you're very gently resisting still, and that's what's being experienced as painful. Even to not want to feel a certain way is resistance.

I can't seem to naturally feel the joy of the Self when I attempt meditative self-inquiry or when I attempt to release my attachments and aversions. I'm worried that I'm doing something wrong.

I experienced the same problem, and I think most people on this path do as well. For me, it was always an issue of my trying to conceptualize "the Self." Our beingness, or our "Self," is truly in a class of its own — everything else that does exist, or could exist, exists objectively. It can be looked at, pointed to, defined in space or time, etc. The Self is not an object. Thus, it's not something you can enjoy in the way you'd enjoy anything else. When you hear people discuss the joys of the Self, your natural inclination is to try and enjoy your beingness as you would other things in your life. But you don't have any reference for that kind of enjoyment because no other kind exists. This is all a long way of saying, don't worry about feeling the joys of the Self. It's not something you can actively pursue or correct when you aren't doing it. Over time, as your understanding progresses, you'll relax into the enjoyment very naturally and without effort.

Is love supposed to be felt as a physical sensation? Assuming the answer's yes, how do I feel more love? I've tried Lester's method of squaring all with love, saying, "Can I change this to love?" And it often works wonders. But sometimes, after I get myself into a high state of very intense love, filling my body with warm sensations, I experience a sort of withdrawal afterward.

Lester made a distinction between human love (love as an active emotion, the way we typically think about it) and divine love. In his descrip-

145

tion, divine love is a complete acceptance and allowing. To love someone divinely is to allow them to shine in your consciousness exactly as they are, with no desire to change or manipulate them. It's a very passive state and different than what most of us think of as love. So when Lester squared all with love, he wasn't saying ,"Oh I love that this terrible thing happened, or I love this person who hurt me." He was just releasing all his reactions, which in turn allowed everything to shine fully in him.

When I do self-inquiry, I can see that I'm at least my awareness, rather than being my body or my mind. But I can't seem to get the experiential realization that I'm all beingness, that I'm all awareness.

This is another area where it's difficult to conceptualize and thus not worth stressing over. But here is something that may help. Rather than try to project or expand yourself outward to include all others, try to disidentify with your ego first. If you go in the other direction, you have to slowly grow your sense of self until it contains everything. If you stop identifying as "little i", the automatic consequence is your identification with everything and everyone.

Are there any prerequisites to the releasing process which I may need to check off prior to proceeding with it?

No prerequisites to releasing. Anyone can do it, and anyone should do it, no matter their current state.

About misidentifying myself with my ego: for what duration would you recommend doing so? Should I do so indefinitely un-

til (possibly days later) I experience a feeling/knowing that it's indeed a misidentification? Or should I do it just for a moment before returning to the question, "To whom is this thought?"

I'd say remind yourself to do it often in an attempt to do it indefinitely. It'll be really hard to stay properly identified at all times starting out, but there should be a gradual correction that takes place, whereby you more and more frequently identify as awareness even when you're not reminding yourself to. It's kind of like building any habit.

If I understand it right, you have to presuppose that any answer the mind gives you is something that cannot be the truth about yourself because the Self is just behind the mind. And that's why we ask, "To whom is this thought?" But wouldn't the logic be circular? When I call every answer the mind gives "limited" and reject it, the only possible answer remaining would be that I am the (unlimited) all.

There's no great answer to this. In short, yes, the process you describe would be circular. The best way I've seen it put is that while the mind can't undo itself via thought, it can point you in the right direction. Jean Klein, a teacher I quite like, spoke often about inquiring to a point where there is no possible answer — a point at which all activity of the mind ceases. This point, paradoxically, is your answer. So don't get hung up. Inquire in a way that feels natural and productive, and you'll continue moving in the right direction.

How would you reconcile Lester's different definitions of divine love? I believe he gave these four at least: 1) complete acceptance and allowing; 2) wanting the other person to have what the other

person wants; 3) total selflessness, giving with no thought of receiving; and 4) identifying with the other person. They don't all make sense to me, and they also seem to contradict each other.

It's important to remember that Lester was teaching to different people at different levels of understanding all the time. So, his specific phraseology of these definitions of love were likely just an attempt to communicate to different types of minds. I think you can see the common thread between the definitions and any disparity can just be understood as being a consequence of the limitations of language.

I do think that all these definitions encourage us to avoid further reinforcing our ego limitations. Lester puts a great emphasis on focusing on others; this is likely because so long as we're focused on our own limitations, love cannot really flow. Acceptance, typically, is directed "outward" toward others — though self-acceptance is important, too.

I also encourage you to ask yourself, "Are these definitions contradictory?" I understand your gut instinct in saying that, but look a little deeper. Is there really a difference between the complete acceptance of someone as they are, wanting for them what they want for themselves, and being totally selfless in working toward their happiness with no expectation of receiving in return? Even more importantly, are all three of these positions not the same positions that most of us take up in regard to our limited selves? So therefore, would holding any of these positions be different from identifying with the other?

Just for illustration, let's say a completely selfless woman named Mary Sue is trying to manifest a relationship with Sean. Sean had just told Mary that he doesn't want to be with her because he could only ever see himself loving his abusive ex. But Mary loves

Sean selflessly, and so she wants a relationship with him because she believes she's uniquely able to make him happy. She doesn't care whether she's loved back by him or not. So, would the loving decision be for Mary to manifest a relationship with Sean? Then Sean wouldn't get what he consciously wants (a relationship with his abusive ex), but rather what he subconsciously wants (happiness and love). Or would the loving decision be for Mary to desire and manifest Sean to get what he consciously wants (a relationship with his ex) but miss out on what he subconsciously wants (happiness and love)?

The Mary/Sean question is a very interesting one. I think the answer hinges on the idea that Mary feels she has the ability to make Sean uniquely happy. At the level of mind, I think it's undeniable that this might be valid. Some interactions will simply lead to "objectively" (in a modern moral sense) better outcomes. They'll lead to less net suffering. But, at the same time, Mary's compulsion to act, to impose her will on the world in some way to improve it, is a denial of the inherent perfection of beingness and, thus, a product of her own misunderstanding. Don't get me wrong — I'm not saying we should never act in the world, and I'm not saying we shouldn't always try and act in ways that lead to positive outcomes in a common sense way.

But the truth of the matter is Mary has no power to make the world better or worse. Beingness is perfect, and thus, the world (a manifestation of beingness) is perfect as well. I think Lester's advice to Mary might differ depending on her level of understanding. The highest advice would be to recognize the innate perfection of beingness and allow that to manifest with no intervention. In this case, even though no intentional "manifesting" of a specific outcome is going on, by holding perfection in mind, she'd have immense power to create an outcome that benefits everyone. If she were at a lower level of understanding, I think he'd tell her to release on

149

her holding Sean in danger of being made to suffer by his ex and on her need to be with Sean to somehow improve her own life. I don't think he'd advise "forcing" a manifestation of Sean being with her if it's not what he wants, even if he doesn't want it because of subconscious hang-ups. That's his obstacle to overcome — we have to be careful not to impose ourselves in an attempt to better the world on our own terms.

Do people "create" their own abuse? What about children?

As pertains to children (and even adults) being harmed or abused, I don't think they "created" their circumstance in some direct way. As in, I don't think they're to blame — at all.

Rather, I believe we can get swept up in the manifestations of others to the degree that we accept or participate in those manifestations. Children are more or less blank slates — this why it's so important to nurture and protect them until they're at a point in development where positive beliefs and feelings have built up. Because of this a child can get caught in the manifestation of someone else's fear/anger through no fault of their own.

This said, once the situation has come to pass and the child grows up, they have the power to go back and let go of the beliefs that were forced into them. It might be a painful process, but if the negative feelings are left unaddressed they will continue to manifest going forward. It's not fair and it's not an issue of the abused person being to blame, but nevertheless I think it's the solution to the suffering. Unfortunately though, we see that many people who suffered the evil of others continue to live lives where that evil perpetuates itself through their having internalized it

Section VI: Techniques

It's Time To Practice

As promised, we're now going to enter into the section of the book that deals with exercises and techniques that can aid you in your conscious creation. While I truly believe that the best way to make progress in manifestation is to internalize all the theoretical material we covered in previous sections of the book, I also know for a fact that to be able to sit down with a set directive and put everything we've learned into practice is immensely valuable in its own right. As Lester was fond of saying, "Any aid that helps you is a good aid — be it Gatorade."

These techniques will be divided into three categories: those that help you understand the metaphysical basis of conscious creation, those that help you learn to release more effectively, and those that help you access and implement your desired states of knowing. As always, I encourage you to experiment with different tools and techniques until you find the ones that work for you. All of us will have different directives that appeal to us.

The Metaphysical

Move Your Awareness

Most people have a tendency to localize their consciousness at a specific point in space. Typically, this point is on the forehead, right between the eyes. As a consequence of this localization, it can be difficult to buy into the idea that we are the consciousness underlying all objects (body/mind included) because it feels as if we exist at such a specific point. This exercise will aid us in breaking that habit.

1. Sit down in a quiet, comfortable place and observe your surroundings passively. There's no need to focus on any specific sight or sound — just take everything in in as relaxed a fashion as possible.

2. Assuming you naturally localize your awareness in the forehead, shift that point of origin a few inches downward to the tip of your nose. Note — your goal isn't to look down at your nose; it's to feel as if the "center" of your being sits at this location.

3. Now, shift your awareness further downward to your heart. Continue to sit comfortably and observe. Does the texture of your experience change when you localize yourself in the chest as opposed to the forehead?

4. Shift your awareness until it is localized about six inches above your head. Take your time with this one — you're probably not used to moving your point of origin outside the body. Again, notice if your experience feels different from a different vantage point.

5. Place your awareness in the far corner of your room. It can be helpful to imagine your eyes as cameras that are relaying information back to you at your new, far-off vantage point. The same goes for any of the other senses — you're sitting at a mission control desk wherever you choose to localize your awareness and can remotely access all the sensory organs.

6. Place your awareness high in the sky, like a satellite.

7. Place your awareness at the back of the head, "behind the world," so to speak. It should almost feel as if the entire world is on a screen in front of you, but there's nothing behind you.

8. Place your awareness "under" the world. Now, instead of projecting the world out in front of you, feel as if it is projected above you. Remember that your body should feel part of the projection.

9. Continue experimenting by moving your awareness around to all different points in space, or even "outside" of space, as we did in the previous two points.

Our goal is to recognize that the apparent localization of our consciousness is not based on any concrete reality and is simply a deeply ingrained habit. Our awareness is non-local; in actuality, it doesn't exist at any point in time or space, as time and space exist in awareness, not the other way around.

Where Does Experience Occur?

As a consequence of our habitually locating ourselves at a specific place in space, we are also conditioned to organize the world in terms of subject/object relationships.

1. Sit down and focus on an object at some distance from yourself. It can be a picture hanging on the far wall, a tree in the yard, or an airplane flying 30,000 feet overhead.

2. Come up with a general estimate of how far away your object is.

3. Ask now how it is you came up with that estimate. How do you know how far away the object is?

4. Once you've settled on an answer, ask the question again — this time, though, formulate an answer that doesn't rely on reference to other objects. So, if you are looking at a lamp in the far corner of the room, how do you know it is 15 feet away without saying, "Well, the table is about three feet away, and there's about four times as much space between me and the table as there is between the table and the lamp, so it must be about 15 feet away..."

5. Reset yourself and pick a new object.

6. Before you try estimating the distance between you and your new object, ask, "Where do I experience this object?" So, despite there being an apparent distance between you and the object, where is it you actually experience the object?

7. Upon some investigation, it should become apparent that you experience the object "here." It's probably not clear exactly where "here" is, but that's okay.

8. Now, compare your new object with the original one you chose. Despite their seeming to exist at distinct points in space, where do you experience both of them?

9. You experience both objects "here." And what about the distance between the two objects? Where do you experience that? You experience that distance "here," as well.

10. As you've been thinking this exercise over, where have your thoughts been occurring? Do they exist at some distance from you? Or are they always experienced here?

11. Try and think of anything that could be experienced in some place other than right here.

After some time spent mulling over point 11, it should become clear that nothing could ever be experienced somewhere other than right "here." But if everything is experienced "here," why is it impossible to pin down exactly where "here" is? Well, because "here" is nowhere — nowhere in time or space, at least. This exercise helps guide us to the realization that because everything is experienced "here" and that "here" has no apparent location, then time and space must exist inside of "here." This is what we mean when we say awareness underlies all reality.

Who Is The "Thinker" Of My Thoughts?

In addition to physically localizing ourselves, we localize ourselves mentally.

1. Think of an animal. It can be the first one that comes to mind or one you settle on after deliberating between a bunch of options.

2. Ask yourself, "At what point did I decide which animal I was going to settle on?"

3. Once you've identified the point at which you made your decision, ask, "Why did I choose to settle at that moment and not continue thinking?"

4. Reset yourself. Clear your mind. Sit quietly until a thought arises organically.

5. Ask yourself, "Why did that thought arise and not some other thought?" Did you choose that thought? Did you scan through an infinite ocean of potential thoughts before plucking out one in particular? Or did it just appear spontaneously?

6. Where did your thought arise out of?

7. Now that I've directed your attention to a number of other questions, where did that initial thought disappear to?

8. If I were to tell you I had a magic thought laser, and I'd beamed it at your head when you started engaging in this exercise in order to make you choose the animal you chose, would you be able to disprove my claim through any direct evidence? Meaning, beyond saying "magic thought lasers don't exist," can you come up with any evidence that proves "you" were in control of the thought you chose and that it wasn't beamed into your head?

9. Continuing along the same line of questioning, would you be able to prove to anyone (yourself included) that you are responsible for any thought you've ever had? Were I to come out and say I've had my

thought laser pointed in your direction for your entire life, could you come up with any evidence to the contrary?

10. If you were to never have another thought again for the rest of your life, would you disappear?

The purpose of this exercise is not to delve into a debate over the existence of free will. It simply serves to illuminate the following: though we often consider ourselves to be the "thinker" of our thoughts (the fact that we refer to them as "my" thoughts is evidence of this), nothing in our experience actually points to that being the case. Thoughts arise, yes, but they arise out of the void and disappear back into the void without our intervention. Even if I were to say, "I'm going to think about X instead of Y," that thought, too, arises out of nowhere like every other thought does.

But just because thoughts arise out of nowhere doesn't mean they arise out of pure, empty nothingness. If you think back to our previous exercise, it's already been established that something exists in nowhere, outside of time and space. That something is you, awareness. In the same way that all objects we experience, we experience "here," all thoughts arise "here" and "now" despite apparently being born out of nowhere.

We can actually ride this wave even further. If a thought arises out of nowhere, out of what could it be constructed? Presumably, anything that arrives from nowhere must be made out of nothing, right? If a thought was made out of some combination of "things," then those things would have had to exist "somewhere" previously. Because we've established that our thoughts must arise out of the nowhere that is consciousness, then they must also be made out of the nothing ("no thing") that is consciousness. And if we analyze our experience, "no thing" is a pretty apt description of awareness. It is not a "thing" — it's not an object the way a tree or a thought is an object — but nevertheless awareness "is." It's the ultimate subject in which all "things" arise.

These exercises bring us right back to our very first chapter of the book — to our zeroth principle. Consciousness is the only reality. It exists nowhere and is made out of nothing, yet it's the only thing we can be certain exists. Because time, space, and all objects (gross or subtle) are born out of the "nowhere" and "nothing" that is awareness, so too must time, space, and all objects be made out of awareness. Consciousness is the fundamental aspect of reality, just as sand is the fundamental reality of the beach on which you build sand castles.

Releasing

If the last chunk of metaphysical exercises seemed totally nonsensical to you, don't fret. As all those ideas are allowed to marinate in your brain over time, they'll start to make sense. And if they don't, you'll be no worse off for it. I don't have the slightest understanding of how an engine is built, but I get in my car every day and the engine runs fine. Just because you don't understand the metaphysical basis of conscious creation doesn't mean you won't be able to employ it effectively.

On that note, let's dive into the releasing-centric exercises.

What Don't I Want To Think About?

Everyone can relate to the experience of having some memory we really don't want to think about. If you're just getting started with releasing, don't feel pressure to jump right into some horrific tragedy that occurred in your past on this exercise. Start with the unpleasant, albeit benign, then work up to the big stuff. Maybe the time you tripped and fell in front of the entire cafeteria, then had to sit there with mashed potatoes all over your face as 500 kids pointed and laughed at you. Maybe the time a guy you liked leaned in for a first kiss, and you sneezed in his face. Something that makes you cringe.

1. Allow the cringe-worthy memory to play out in your mind completely free of resistance. That's not to say you can't feel embarrassed or ashamed or whatever, but let your feelings arise organically and don't actively interfere with them.

2. Run the memory again. And again. And again. Remember, non-resistance is key here. If every time you run the memory you get more and more lost in the negative feelings, take a break and return back later.

3. As you progress through this process, gently take note of how your emotional reactions change over time. Do they lessen as you go? Do different parts of the memory feel more or less uncomfortable as you repeat the exercise? Are different emotions triggered on repetition ten than were on repetition one?

4. Now, take extra care to relax as you continue looping your uncomfortable memory. Unclench your jaw, open your hands, and let your body sink into whatever you're sitting/laying on until it's almost completely limp. Even though we're participating in a mental exercise, our bodies take it upon themselves to play a part in the resistance process by tensing up.

5. As you relax more and more, are you able to "feel" your way past the surface-level negative reactions and arrive at something deeper? If your initial reaction was to feel anxious and afraid in response to your memory, can you ease your way toward a deeper feeling of guilt or shame? Don't feel compelled to "make up" a feeling that isn't there — maybe fear is as deep as the memory goes. But if there's more searching to do, try and relax as you go deeper.

6. Can you get so relaxed and be so accepting of your uncomfortable memory that your emotional reaction to it spontaneously "shuts off?"

We're accomplishing two things with this exercise. First, we're learning to set up a healthy distance between ourselves and our emotional reactions. By taking note of how we feel and how feelings change over time, we become more capable of dealing with them.

Secondly, and far more importantly, we're practicing the release process in its purest form. If you had any lack of clarity about how releasing is meant to function at the most basic level, congratulations, you just experienced it. If you didn't experience the spontaneous "shutting off" of negative reactions, that's okay — you'll get there with some practice.

A useful analogy for understanding releasing is that of stretching a tight muscle. Say I can't touch my toes — I'd describe this as being a result of my "tight" hamstrings, but that doesn't paint the entire picture. Muscles don't really get "tight" in the way that a guitar string gets "tight" as I begin to tune it — muscle tightness is as much neurological as it is skeletomuscular. As I move my body from day to day, week to week, and year to year, my brain begins to acclimate itself to the ranges of motion in which I typically operate. If I never engage in any activity that forces the hamstrings to lengthen to the extent that they will if I were to touch my toes, and then suddenly I attempt to do so, my brain goes, "Woah, woah, woah buddy — you're gonna hurt yourself." It reflexively contracts the hamstring to prevent me from entering into a range of motion that might be dangerous. As a result, a major part of improving flexibility is training your brain to lessen these reflexive muscle contractions so you can carefully enter new ranges of motion.

Free flexibility lesson aside (note that I am not a doctor or physical therapist, am not offering medical advice, and cannot be held responsible if you tear your hamstrings off the bone in an excited attempt to touch your toes), releasing works by a similar process. Your emotional reactions are reflexive. For years and years, you've been allowing them to keep you from facing any thought or knowing you deemed to be unapproachable. As a result, they've become very efficient at their job. If you barrel into the releasing process like a bull in a china shop, you're going to immediately trigger your emotional defense mechanisms. There'll be nothing you can do mentally to get around them in the same way that you can't mentally turn off your stretch reflex.

The secret is to relax. Don't force things that aren't coming. Don't manipulate or cajole your emotions. Just allow your uncomfortable memory to shine fully in the light of awareness. The second you stop resisting the process, the surface-level defense mechanisms click off, and you'll slip down to the next layer of emotional defenses. Rinse and repeat this "allowing" until you slip down to the root issue, and at that point, it'll release spontaneously. No effort required.

Memory Surfing

One of the great things about releasing is that I don't have to go one-by-one through every single negative experience I've ever had in order to set myself free. Because there's a pattern to our emotional defense mechanisms, I can neutralize hundreds or even thousands of negative memories in a single swipe when I address and release the underlying pattern of emotions. It's kind of like pulling a weed out at the roots.

1. Sit in a quiet, comfortable place and do your best to clear your mind. Choose a negative experience you'd like to address and call it up into mind.

2. As you allow this memory up into awareness completely, pay special attention to the feelings it triggers.

3. Instead of repeating the memory, once you've gone over it once or twice, allow it to drift back out of your mind, then remain in a quiet state of meditation for a while.

4. Whenever the next memory arises, carry out the same process. Allow it to shine fully in awareness, then let it drift away on its own accord.

5. If the same memory spontaneously replays itself over and over again, that's fine. If you let a memory drift away, then the same memory resurfaces a few minutes later, that's fine too.

6. Continue "surfing" this wave of memories for a while. It's important to remember that non-resistance is still important here. You shouldn't be actively turning your back on a memory that wants to be acknowledged – just allowing the memories to come and go as they please.

After spending some time on this exercise, you'll notice that memories aren't arising randomly — they'll all be connected by feeling. I might start thinking about the jerk who cut me off in traffic today but end up 50 years in the past thinking about how my neighbor threw my G.I. Joe in a lake when we were six. All the memories I surf in between will likely have been instances of people satisfying their spur-of-the-moment desires at my expense. And what I might find is that the pattern of responding with anger to these events began a long time ago when I was grief-stricken over the loss of my G.I. Joe and didn't want to face the fact that my beloved toy was gone forever, so I resolved to repress that knowledge by getting angry.

If I can release on that deep-seated memory, I can also free myself from every instance of the "person does something at my expense, so I get angry" pattern.

Connect The Dots

One of Lester's breakthrough realizations on his journey was that underlying all AGFLAP is the desire for approval and control, and underlying the desire for approval and control is the fear of death. In the same way that we might develop a pattern of responding angrily to situations as an emotional defense mechanism, there's a pattern to the things that upset us in the first place. When I feel disapproved of or like I've lost control, I respond by feeling apathy, grief, fear, lust, anger, or pride; the reason these emotional defense mechanisms are necessary is because lack of approval and lack of control make me feel existentially threatened — they make me feel like I might die. As out there as it might seem to suggest that being yelled at by your boss somehow ties back to an innate fear of death, if you really think about it, that kind of makes sense.

In tribal times, were you to lose the approval of your immediate society, you'd be outcast and would die. Similarly, if you were thrust into a situation that you could not control — if a grizzly bear came barrelling through your camp — you'd also be at risk of dying. So it's not a significant leap to suggest that our deep desire for approval and control is linked to our fear of death and that negative emotional reactions are generally triggered in situations where we feel disapproved of or like we don't have any control. This brings us to our exercise.

1. Call to mind any uncomfortable memory. As you allow it up into awareness and all the associated emotions begin to play out, ask yourself, "Is a feeling of disapproval or lack of control what triggered my initial reaction?"

2. Pick a different memory that has a distinct emotional texture to it. If the first memory made you angry, pick one that makes you fearful, guilty, or ashamed. Repeat the process. Was your emotional reaction somehow connected to your desire for approval or control?

3. Repeat as many times as feels right.

This is perhaps the simplest of exercises you can engage in. And while I'd never put words in your mouth, I'm fairly certain that you'll come to find many of your reactions are triggered by feelings of disapproval or lack of control, then ultimately a fear of death.

As for what this means in terms of your releasing process? Lester often encouraged people to release specifically on approval and control so as to expedite their progress. In theory, if you can release your desire for approval, 50+ percent of your negative emotional reactions should release with it. And if you were to release your fear of death directly, everything would go with it; you'd be totally free.

This is something you can experiment with. I think generally, it's better to start with a more targeted approach and work up to the big stuff. If you've never released before and you go right for approval, the mental stretch reflex might be too strong to overcome. It may prove impossible to relax yourself to the point that you're able to allow the feeling up with no resistance and make progress. But as you move along on your path, it'll certainly become advisable to start releasing things in bigger and bigger chunks.

Accessing Desired States

Techniques and exercises really start to shine when it comes to accessing your desired states. There are innumerable ways you can do it, so definitely don't feel required to stop with the ones I list here. It's also worth noting that you don't have to be fully released to start implementing desired-state techniques. The two practices should be engaged with in tandem. As you release more and more emotional baggage, your desired state exercises will become more and more powerful.

State Akin To Sleep

Everyone's favorite manifestation technique, as initially taught by Neville Goddard. This is ol' reliable when it comes to getting into your desired state of knowing.

1. Lay down in bed, close your eyes, and imagine in vivid detail the object/experience you'd like to manifest. Feel it in vivid detail like it's really happening. Maybe you're imagining shaking your boss's hand as he congratulates you on your new promotion. Feel his hand gripping yours. See his office in perfect detail. Smell his cologne. Hear the sounds

of your coworkers typing away at their desks behind you. Make it as real as is humanly possible.

2. Once you get to the end of this visualization, repeat the process. Take care to preserve every bit of detail as you do.

3. Loop this scene over and over again as you begin to drift off into sleep. At a certain point, you'll find yourself in the twilight zone between wakefulness and dreaming, and the visualization will really take on an incredible reality.

4. Keep the repetition going until you fall asleep.

The classics are classic for a reason. This is a great method of familiarizing yourself with your desired state of knowing for a set period of time every day. I also think there's immense value in visualizing while in the half-awake, half-asleep twilight zone — for whatever reason, accessing your desired state of knowing here seems to be tremendously effective in changing your baseline, unconscious state even when you're awake and thinking of other things.

I Remember When

Another Neville Goddard go-to.

1. Imagine being with a friend and telling them, "I remember when... *I was broke and thought my art career would never take off. Now I'm here with my own gallery and am selling so many paintings I can barely keep up...* *I was so lonely and couldn't find the right relationship. Now I'm getting married to the love of my life, and things couldn't be better...*I would spend all day looking at pictures of that Ferrari online and had no idea how I'd ever get my hands on one. Now I get up every day and drive it to work.*"

169

2. Whatever your current unfavorable circumstance is, insert it into the above prompt. If you're poor and want to be rich, tell your friend you remember when you were poor. If you're single and want to be married, tell your friend you remember being single."

3. Eventually, you don't even have to imagine you're talking to a friend. You can just talk to yourself mentally. I remember when...

By talking about your current circumstances in the past tense, you're (by default) entering into the state of your desire fulfilled.

Affirmation

Affirmation is perhaps the simplest method of implementing a new state of subconscious knowing. It's also the most effective of the so-called "brute force" techniques.

1. Come up with a short phrase or sentence that speaks to the outcome you wish to see fulfilled. Make sure it's constructed in the present tense. Ex. "I am wealthy," "I am loved," "I am admired."

2. Repeat your phrase as often as possible throughout the day, either out loud or in your mind.

Repetition is the name of the game here. Don't be afraid to set lofty goals — can you repeat your affirmation 200 times today? 400? More? In some sense, we're working backward with this method. Instead of directly changing our state of knowing and allowing that to give rise to new thoughts, we're interjecting new thoughts with such a frequency that our state of knowing is forced to change. This is particularly useful in that it doesn't require much thought or effort — once you get into the rhythm of affirming, the process will run on autopilot.

3, 6, 9 Method

Similar to affirmation.

1. Construct a sentence or phrase that describes what you're trying to manifest. Again, make sure it's in the present tense — so, instead of saying, "I want a big house," say "I have a big house."

2. In the morning, write your phrase down three times.

3. Throughout the day, write your phrase six more times.

4. Before bed, write your phrase out nine more times.

Not much to say here. This is a simple and easy technique aimed at re-entering your chosen state of knowing periodically throughout the day.

Vision Boards

A classic technique that has made its way into mainstream self-help circles.

1. Print out pictures that you associate with the state of your desire fulfilled and post/pin/paste them on a poster board.

2. Hang the board up somewhere that you'll see often.

Your vision board should serve to passively remind you of your desire throughout the day. Even when you aren't specifically focusing on it, merely catching a glimpse as you go through your normal routine will lead to shifts in your subconscious state.

Reorganize Your Life

This is a fantastic technique I first heard described in Rhonda Byrne's book *The Secret*.

1. Take stock of your life as you currently live it. What kind of things do you do habitually on a day-to-day basis?

2. Consider how your day-to-day life will look once your desire has been fulfilled.

3. Try to reconcile any differences between the two days. For example, if you are trying to manifest a relationship, but you normally sleep in the center of your bed, start sleeping on one side of the mattress — basically, make room for your partner. If right now you work at a fast food restaurant but are trying to land a powerful corporate job, instead of waking up in the morning and hanging out in pajamas until your shift starts, get up and put on a suit.

You might feel like a goofball sitting around watching TV in a suit or setting out an extra plate and silverware for a partner that doesn't exist yet, but it's the spirit that counts here. Your goal should be to close the gap between how you live now and how you plan to live in the future.

Pruning Shears Of Revision

This technique, as described by Neville Goddard, is kind of a combination of releasing and accessing a desired state.

1. Think back to a situation that didn't play out how you hoped it would. Maybe your boss telling you the company decided not to approve your raise, or your former partner telling you they think it'd be best to see other people.

2. In your mind's eye, go back and "revise" the unwanted memory. Visualize your boss telling you the company had approved your raise, or your former partner telling you how happy they are with the relationship.

3. Repeat this process until the new revised memory takes on a reality similar to the original suboptimal memory.

We're doing the work on clearing out old, unwanted feelings by way of inserting preferred ones. If you have a lot of intense negative feelings about a past scenario, it might be necessary to work on releasing first, before you start revising.

Method Acting

Method actors like Robert De Niro and Daniel Day Lewis are as adept at accessing and embodying new states of knowing as anyone on the planet. We can learn from the ways in which they prepare for roles.

1. Take some time to explore how you will feel when your desired outcome has manifested. Your state of knowing might only be subtly different now than it will be when your desire is fulfilled, so really key in on little differences in feeling. Will you carry yourself differently or walk with a slightly more confident gait? Will your voice be a bit clearer and more commanding?

2. Start doing things "in character" as the version of yourself who's had your desire fulfilled. When you brush your teeth in the morning, do it in character. When you drive to work, be in character. Again, the difference in how you feel when you're "in character" might be ever so slight compared to how you feel typically, but we still want to make sure we're embodying those differences.

3. When you go out into the world and interact with people, do so in character. If you're checking out at the grocery store, don't do so as the version of yourself who is broke; do it "in character" as the version of yourself who is rich.

This is a good way to gamify the accessing of your desired state. Though you might not act differently or say different things when you're in character talking to the receptionist at your office, how you feel internally as you do so should be different. Focus on all the little nuances.

Section VII:
Further Study

The Teachers Who Helped Guide Me

Isaac Newton once said, "If I've seen further, it is by standing on the shoulders of giants." Because I can't claim to have seen quite as far (and certainly not further) than the many spiritual giants who came before me, I might revise the statement to, "If I've seen any distance at all, it is by the grace of giants who plucked me up, placed me on their shoulders, and offered a more pleasant view." I know; my version isn't as catchy.

The bottom line is that my understanding of conscious creation could never have developed were it not for the grace of the many teachers from whom I've learned over the years. Some I've mentioned throughout the book, some I haven't, but all played a part in helping me progress on my path. I'd like to direct your attention now to the many who helped me so that they might help you.

I think it's worth noting that those I list below may not agree with all of my ideas — some of them don't speak at all about conscious creation and thus might consider a book on the subject to be nonsensical and meaningless. But everyone mentioned provided me with some form or another of spiritual insight, so I recommend you study them all.

Lester Levenson

The creator of the release technique and the program that has gone on to be known as the Sedona Method. Lester was a normal man who lived much of his life in discomfort before forging his own path to enlightenment. Lester's teachings are as near and dear to my heart as any — his book *Keys To The Ultimate Freedom* and the many hours of audio recordings from his days of teaching (available online) were instrumental to my growth.

Neville Goddard

A pioneer of the new thought movement who established many ideas relating to the "law of assumption." Neville wrote countless books and gave many lectures relating to manifestation. A number of his creation techniques have been discussed previously.

Rhonda Byrne

Author of *The Secret, The Power, The Magic, and The Greatest Secret* (among others). Rhonda is responsible for a large portion of the moder- day interest in the "law of attraction" and manifestation.

Joseph Murphy

A contemporary of Neville Goddard, who had an equal impact on advancing ideas relating to conscious creation and manifestation. Murphy places a heavy emphasis on the importance of affirmation in reconstituting the subconscious mind.

Rupert Spira

A modern teacher of Advaita Vedanta (a school of non-dual thought). Rupert is perhaps the world's greatest communicator of complex and unintuitive metaphysical ideas. He's written an entire library of books worth reading — among them, *Being Aware Of Being Aware* and *Being Myself*. He holds in-person retreats around the world.

Francis Lucille

Rupert's teacher and another revered voice in the non-dual space. Francis also holds retreats and has penned books, including *Eternity Now* and *The Perfume Of Silence*.

Laura Lucille

A student of Lester Levenson and the Sedona method; wife to Francis. Laura produces online content and is available for one-on-one coaching.

Hale Dwoskin

A student of Lester Levenson and the founder of Sedona Training Associates. Hale's book, *The Sedona Method* (A New York Times Bestseller) draws directly from the wisdom he developed during many years spent studying alongside Lester.

Dr. David Hawkins

Dr. Hawkins was yet another student of Lester's and the author of many enlightening books, *Letting Go* being the most famous among them. Before embarking on his spiritual journey, Dr. Hawkins practiced as a world-renowned psychiatrist.

Eckhart Tolle

New York Times bestselling author of books including *The Power Of Now* and *A New Earth*. Eckhart offers in-person seminars and online courses relating to all things spirituality.

Martin Brofman

A world-renowned spiritual teacher/healer who authored *Anything Can Be Healed*. Martin embarked on his spiritual path after being diagnosed with an inoperable tumor. In addition to overcoming his own health problems, he gave tens of thousands of others the tools and knowledge necessary to overcome theirs.

Jean Klein

Teacher to Francis Lucille and author of books including *The Ease Of Being*, *The Book Of Listening*, and *I AM*. In addition to his work as a spiritual teacher, Jean was a medical doctor and classically trained musician.

John Wheeler

A modern teacher of non-duality. John's books (including *You Were Never Born* and *Awakening To The Natural State*) are among the clearest guides possible to the basics of non-dual thought.

Vadim Zeland

Author of *Reality Transurfing*. Vadim presents an enlightening model of reality creation meant to help readers live better, more fulfilling lives.

Sailor Bob Adamson

Teacher of Advaita Vedanta and mentor to John Wheeler. Sailor Bob's books *What's Wrong With Right Now Unless You Think About It* and *Presence-Awareness* communicate non-dual ideas in a simple but extraordinarily meaningful way.

Dr. Joe Dispenza

Another New York Times bestselling author responsible for books including *You Are The Placebo* and *Becoming Superhuman*. Dr. Dispenza offers in-person lectures, online programs, and a number of other spiritual resources in addition to his books.

José Silva

Creator and author of *The Silva Mind Control Method*, a meditative technique designed to help practitioners enact positive changes to themselves and the world around them. Much of Martin Brofman's early work was influenced by his involvement in the Silva Method.

This list is by no means exhaustive — the world is full of insightful spiritual teachers who can help deepen your understanding of conscious creation. By studying the people I've mentioned here, I'm sure you'll find your way to other great thinkers who can guide you on your personal journey.

Conclusion

I Wish You The Best Of Luck

At the time of writing, it's been almost two decades since I first stumbled upon the concept of conscious creation. Something about the idea that we create our reality always rang true to me — even if I couldn't pinpoint why exactly that was the case. As a great teacher once said, truth strikes us not as newfound knowledge, but as knowledge we'd long ago forgotten and have now come to remember. When it comes to manifestation, this was certainly my experience. Conscious creation was a truth I'd known all along, but one that had taken some years to remember.

Even with this being the case, my journey wasn't linear. As years passed, I travelled through peaks and valleys of understanding. I'd have periods rife with insight followed by long stretches where I felt so lost that I'd never find my way again. But through it all, I persisted. I continued to study, continued to read, and most importantly of all, I continued to think deeply about the nature of my own experience.

This book is the product of all that time spent in thought. And though my personal journey will not serve as a substitute for yours, I hope the insights I've come to might serve to guide you on your path in the same way that the insights of others served to guide me.

If you take anything away from what I've written, let it be this: You have the power to make your life better. Life might not feel heavenly today or tomorrow, but if you continue to work toward improving the lens through which you view the world, things will improve. You'll find more and more happiness, and one day, you'll wake up knowing that you have the power to create a life beyond that of your wildest dreams. I can say this because I experienced it — and I know that one day you will too.

I wish you the best of luck.